One of Them

One of Them

Chapters from
A Passionate Autobiography

BY

ELIZABETH HASANOVITZ

Boston and New York
HOUGHTON MIFFLIN COMPANY
1918

Published August 1918

To the memory of

ROBERT G. VALENTINE

who extended a brotherly hand to me and whose wish to send to the world a message from thousands of us I fulfill with gratitude

and to

S. S. POLAKOFF

my teacher and brother in struggle

ONE OF THEM

CHAPTER I

SUNK in despondency, I had forgotten everything, my surroundings, the hall where the Dramatic Club was meeting, the members of the club, all had vanished in my misery.

"Are you asleep?"

I jumped up. Near me stood Clara, one of the members of the club, who had always shown a friendly interest in me. She recalled me with a start to the present. I was sitting in a dark, low-ceilinged hall, the shelter of our Dramatic Club. Slowly and monotonously the rehearsal had gone; the director, his body reeking with sweat, had repeated to the tenth time the act which failed to please him.

The object of the club was to acquaint the Yiddish public of the East Side of New York with literary dramas, to encourage a better understanding of literature than they could gain from the Yiddish theatres, which usually fed their patrons with the trash common in the theatrical world. The best dramas of Ibsen, Hauptmann, Sudermann, and other modern writers were translated into Yiddish and produced in that small hall by a few idealists who devoted all their spare time and sacrificed a great deal of their earnings for the creation of a literary folk-theatre.

That evening the last rehearsal for the next day's performance had taken place. Confused and puzzled, I had sat through the rehearsal. The poor light in the hall had brought the ceiling still lower, making me sink in deeper despair. Was the play interesting or not, the acting good or bad? I did not see. Where was my enthusiasm gone? What was nagging me so dreadfully?

My mind wandered in dark confusion. Unconsciously, my hand digging in my pocket crumpled a small piece of paper. What was it?

Oh, yes, a two-dollar bill! And the enlightenment came: my only two dollars — all my precious wealth!

Over me swept the past nine weeks — weeks of weary, never-ending search for work. Each day rising with new hope, looking over the advertisements, running from place to place, all fruitless, until, broken with fatigue, I would return home, throw myself on the bed, and spend the rest of the day in the stupor of despair, apathetically gazing at the ceiling.

Most of the advertisements wanted skilled "hands"; others were four-dollar jobs with little chance for advancement. My self-respect would not permit me to slave for four dollars a week.

Nine long, long weeks I looked in vain for a place where I could learn some trade that would in the end pay me more. After a long year of struggle, here I stood more helpless than the day of my arrival in America.

Why had I come to America? What had I accomplished by that historic change in my life?

From the dark brooding that made me unconscious of my surroundings, I was recalled by Clara's kindly voice. The lights were all out, the people all gone.

"Wake up, kid, wake up! It's time to go home. You do not mind if I walk home with you?"

I looked up at her as if I saw her for the first time. A face full of wrinkles, a cut on the lower lip, big, inflamed eyes that looked at me smilingly; a face that I had never liked before looked much pleasanter to me now.

"Why, yes, I shall be glad," I said.

Down we climbed the dark, dirty, creaking staircase, tracing our way along Orchard Street — a small, dirty thoroughfare crowded with push-carts and people. The noise of the elevated trains on Allen Street was deafening, but above the din was a greater noise than usual. Bells were ringing, whistles blowing, the air was full of merriment and joy. Young girls and boys holding feather dusters dipped in some ill-smelling powder or charcoal, smeared the faces of the people as they passed by.

"New Year's Eve! New Year's Eve!" Clara exclaimed joyfully, infected by the merriment of those around her.

To me it was annoying. Could not people enjoy themselves more intelligently? On New Year's Eve in Russia, the peasants usually get drunk and often break the windows of the Yiddish dwellings. Here the young folks were running around screaming like wild animals, tormenting the passers-by.

"You are moody to-night. Cheer up, kid; your boats are not all sunk, are they?"

She was amazed to see me in such a mood, for by nature I was a joyous person and among my friends I made myself very merry, often being the ringleader in all the fun, so that my sufferings for the last nine weeks were not known to any one.

"I think they are, Clara," I answered, clutching my two-dollar bill which so painfully reminded me of my situation.

Her efforts to start a conversation were not successful. I was too tired and discouraged to speak, and silently we reached my door. After wishing each other good-night and a Happy New Year, I climbed up the dark, dirty stairway to the fourth floor and opened the door into a cold, unfriendly room. An old couch, two chairs, a broken white table, and an old, one-time-white dresser furnished the small room. The only window faced a narrow court that never allowed the sunlight to break into my room. My room-mate was absent. I lit the gas.

Lonely and homesick, I paced back and forth from one corner to another, my mind painfully wandering far, far away to my home, now clad in silver white.

H — r-r — roph, h — r-r — roph, h — r-r — roph, h — r-r — roph!

Oh, those sickening sounds from my snoring neighbors! From the windows crowded round the air-shaft they came into my room, driving me almost to distraction. For two months that snoring discord disturbed my peace, irritated my nerves, and kept me awake through the night.

The city clock slowly struck twelve. The New Year had come. More bells ringing, cheerful voices greeting: "Happy New Year! Happy New Year!" came faintly above the other sounds to my room. What had the past year brought to me? And what will the New Year bring? Like a curse the wishes rang in my ears.

Everything began to mingle before me. All the scenes and experiences of the past year chased through my brain: my home, Russia with its persecutions, my departure, my journey, my arrival in America, the factory in Canada where I worked first, my arrival in New York, five weeks of work in a factory in New York, — and then the nine weeks of searching for work. The memories crowded my brain and numbed me with their hopelessness.

Home, home! How I wished to be there, in that spacious living-room with its four windows all opening on the street; at that long table with the older children around it, busy at their tasks; mother seated near the brick oven, bending over a boxful of goose feathers, separating the down, preparing pillows for her daughters' future homes; all awaiting father's return, who after the hard day's work in his school gave private lessons in the evening in order to keep up his "small" family. The younger children playing joyfully on the floor, delighted to play tricks on us, calling, from time to time, "There is father!" and laughing gleefully when they succeeded in making us raise our heads, in vain, to greet our self-sacrificing bread-winner.

Home! To be back in that warm home under mother's devoted caresses; to be sitting with father like a true comrade, discussing with him new plans and methods for the success of our school.

My father was a Hebrew teacher. As only a small proportion of Jews could gain admission into Russian educational institutions, Russian was taught in the Hebrew schools, but secretly, because the Jews were not allowed to teach it without a special license, which they could seldom get. My own small school of girls was also without a license.

I had received my education from private

teachers because I had never been able to get a chance to attend the Russian schools. Jews are permitted to form only five per cent of the total enrollment of pupils in the public and high schools and a decreasing percentage in the higher institutions. Once, when I was ready to pass my examination, my application was rejected because the list of possible applicants was full. The second time the examination was made so difficult that out of sixty girls only fourteen passed, nine Russian and five Yiddish. The rest, all Yiddish girls, failed. Questions absolutely out of the course were put to us. The majority of us knew the prescribed course thoroughly because we were aware of the difficulties the Government created for Jewish students and were prepared for them. Still, we failed.

Those long years of struggle for an education! At fourteen I was already giving lessons to beginners so as to earn money to pay for my books and teachers that I might be less a burden to my father. His highest ambition was to see me get my teacher's diploma, so that we could open a licensed school and stop paying graft to the chief of police, who threatened us continually. Many times the chief and his guards would disturb us in the middle of the day, interrupting our work and frightening the children, who feared the uniforms as if they concealed devils, and who were thrown into frenzy at their approach.

Ghostly pale and shivering as if from a Siberian frost, the children would hastily rid their portfolios of all Russian books and papers, which they would pile together and send flying, pile after pile, across the room and into the cellar, that splendid hiding-place for the crime of stealing a Russian education! After such a visit the rest of the day was spent in the difficult task of assorting the books and papers for their frightened little owners. Each visit of that kind meant a precious twenty-five dollar bill. My father had paid fines several times for my school because I was under age; and even with a diploma, I could not teach until I was twenty-one, so that my father bore all the responsibility.

With my second failure to obtain a diploma, all our hopes, cherished for so many years, began to vanish. The chief of police assailed us more frequently; we were less and less able to fill up his bottomless pocket. After each visit days of misery followed. Many, many times my father and I sat through the night, thinking and thinking how to better our condition, what future to provide for my brothers and sisters. Nothing could be done. Members of the human family, people with brains and ambition, we were not citizens; we were children of the cursed Pale, with our rights limited, the districts in which we could live and the trades and professions we could follow, all prescribed for us. What would become of us? What could we expect?

Fight for liberty, for equal rights? The persecution was so terrible — for one free word one found a home in prison.

"Oh, father, it is suicidal," I would often say.

He would sit downcast, as if guilty for giving life to his children, whose fate like his was to live within the Pale, to be in the hands of the Government dogs, to fear the least drunken moujik who, influenced by the priests, would so often make a sudden attack on the property and sometimes lives of the Yiddish people. They said that they considered it a virtue to rob and kill the enemies of Christ.

Freedom, freedom!

Freedom, I wanted.

"Father," I once said when the family was seated around the table ready for the Sabbath meal, — "father, I have been thinking of myself and of you all, thinking hard for the last three weeks. What will become of me, and of all of us, if we remain in this hole? The future appears so dark to me. I have been thinking, and I have decided that — that — I — shall — go to America."

Thunderstruck by my last words, they all looked at me. The first to break the silence was my mother.

"Are you mad? A young girl — alone — in a far country?" She trembled, tears flowing from her eyes, feeling hurt that I should think of leaving home. Father sat silent, his head hidden in his hands. The youngsters were crying with mother.

"Never let me hear that nonsense again!"

"But, mother, I shall go finally. I do not want to waste my life. I am tired of being condemned to eternal limitations. I want to be free. I shall go to America — a free country, where everybody gets free education. Imagine, mother, free education! I shall earn my living and study in the free evening schools — and when I establish firm ground under my feet, I shall help you and father and the children. Think of the children going to free schools, growing up to be free citizens!"

My mother would not listen. Nor would my father. Except for my younger brother, I had no one's approval. But my determination was strong and the fight began.

For many days my mother's tears would not dry. She would picture to me all the hardships in a far country.

"No matter how bitter life is here, still there is no place like home. What will become of you there — a working-girl?"

My mother could not tolerate the idea that I might become a working-girl. The tradition of a respectable family in our town, no matter how poor, was to keep their daughters at home. The only occupation for girls was either dressmaking or domestic service — the latter being very degrading because of its surroundings, and working-girls were recruited only from the poorest people.

Teaching, to my mother, was something divinely noble, and could have no relation to the prosaic term, "work."

"There will be no one to look after you," she would continue. "I shall live in constant anxiety. I shall not sleep nights thinking that you may not have a warm place to sleep, that you may not have your meals regularly, your laundry done, nor your clothes mended."

Poor mother! Her sensitive heart perceived in advance all the misery that life had prepared for me when I found myself on the other side of the globe.

"But, mother, I am no more a baby. I have passed eighteen and am big enough to take care of myself wherever I am."

"Think of mother and me," father would say. "What will become of us? Do you realize what it means to part with a child? In sorrow or in gladness, we must all be together."

Not succeeding in persuading me to remain, father declared that he would not endorse my passport, and without his consent I could not leave Russia.

Weeks passed. I failed in getting their consent.

As a last resort, I tried a hunger strike.

When after three days of hunger, tired and weakened, I still refused to eat, father brought me the passport.

Then preparations began. Sewing and packing, all dipped in mother's tears.

Then the day of my departure, that forever memorable day! Mother fainting, the children crying, father walking sadly back and forth across the living-room, the house full of neighbors who had come to say good-bye, my pupils with flowers to wish me well. When I was seated in the stage-coach my father jumped up, clutched me in his arms, and bit rather than kissed my cheek. That last scream from my mother's wounded heart as the stage moved off still rings in my ears. A scream from a heart torn, it may be forever, from its dearest and best beloved!

All I left behind me with regret and yet with no regret.

Then the weary days on the train. The third-class coach in which I rode was divided into sections; each section with eight hard benches, four upper and four lower; each bench planned for two passengers to sit, but no place to sleep. During those three days until we reached the seaport, we slept sitting or leaning on our luggage. The great unwashed mass who had occupied these benches before us, sleeping in their clothes and often in their kojuck,[1] had left countless insects behind them, who made our lives miserable. My clothes

[1] Kojuck is a loose gathered overcoat lined with lamb skin — a splendid hiding-place for all sorts of vermin.

were full of vermin when I arrived at Libau. I immediately found a bath-house and cleansed myself from the parasites, but the immigration houses where we stopped were equally infested. Immigrants are treated worse than prisoners, not only in Russia, but also in England. We were driven from one bad place to another still worse. In London, our baggage was opened, our clothes thrown carelessly together with those of the other passengers to be disinfected by steam, then replaced in our trunks, all rolled up and wet. My things were so mussed that I had not even a clean shirt-waist fit to wear on the voyage. The food in the immigration houses was not fit for animals, but we were only immigrants.

On the steamer we travelled steerage to Canada, together with unwashed Russian peasants and a little cleaner German ones. We — a girl friend and myself — were lost among them, like two little wrens in a flock of crows.

It was impossible to sit with them at the table. Not used to knives and forks they would dip their soiled hands into the platter and grab the food, stuffing their mouths, chewing with relish and making a noise that reminded us of pigs around a full trough. We begged the interpreter to bring us some food to our rooms, but he said it was against the rules. For two days I took nothing but a glass of tea, and we spent most of our time on deck.

On the third day I became seasick and did not leave my berth for four days. Our repeated appeal for food in our rooms was always met with the laconic reply, "Them orders is orders — you can't get anything in your rooms." I should have starved had not a gentle Englishman from the third class brought me an orange occasionally. With his help we tipped the interpreter and the porter and "them orders is orders" was forgotten: we had our food in our room. On the seventh day I recovered and spent the remaining seven days on deck or in the third class with the English people, — they were all British in the third class, — who arranged concerts each evening at which we sang.

Two hours before we arrived at Quebec we were held up by quarantine officers. A man in the steerage had contracted typhoid fever, and all the passengers in the steerage and third class were kept in quarantine for another two weeks, held prisoners on a small island in the St. Lawrence and fed with meat filled with worms.

These experiences also I left behind me, and took my first step on the other side of the globe from home, full of hope and ready to endure against anything and everything.

In Canada I was fairly prosperous, but I chafed at the provincialism of its mental atmosphere. My restless mind sought something to interest me, to inspire me, to absorb me.

My second stop, Chicago, was also unsatisfactory, and I decided to try the much-feared New York.

"New York, the devil's nest!" How people tried to warn me, tried to keep me back!

"A girl with no trade, no relations, will soon get lost. Youth and beauty fade there so quickly," they would say.

If my people could not keep me from coming to America, strangers surely could not keep me from coming to New York.

So the last week of September, 1912, I arrived in New York, with eight dollars in my pocket and just one address, given me by the Socialist-Territorialist Party to their New York headquarters.

In truth, I was full of fear all the way, a girl all alone in New York, not knowing the language.

"Nonsense, I am old enough to take care of myself." I tried to quiet my fears as I had tried to quiet my mother's.

When I stepped out of the train at the Grand Central Station, not then completed, a few middle-aged ladies, travellers' guides from the Y.W.C.A., stopped me, asking me if I wished assistance. But not knowing who they were, I looked at them with distrust.

I went out on the street with my heavy suitcase, making my way among the various porters, who offered their assistance, and, seeing my look of suspicion, showed me their badges to reassure me. But I went to a policeman, who put me on a street-car, and I found the office on Delancy Street, where members of the staff received me kindly.

Luckily, I found a job in Brooklyn, in a knitting factory, to sew pockets on sweaters — the same work I had done in Canada. It was the height of the season. Ten dollars a week was considered good pay.

I found a room on Eighth Street; also a roommate. I managed to live on five dollars a week — one dollar for my share of the room rent, three dollars for food, and one dollar for general expenses. The other five I began to save. I wanted to save enough to buy a ticket for my brother so that he might come, and together we might bring the rest of the family.

All went smoothly. I joined the Dramatic Club, satisfying one of my first ambitions — to act. Lectures, readings, all were open to me.

The only thing that bothered me was my shop. It was so different from those in which I had worked before. The atmosphere seemed so common and vulgar. In Canada I had worked with girls whose language I had not understood, while here I worked with Yiddish girls. Their frankness in manner and speech often made me blush and they would tease me. The forelady, an old, shrivelled scold, would display her set of gold teeth as she said: "Looks as if you were only yesterday out of short skirts. H'm! H'm! Still waters run deep." And she would follow me with a hateful look, for the foreman treated me respectfully and she envied me.

"Say, how long do you work in a factory?" she once asked me.

"Only a few months," I answered.

"And I am working in this place for eight years, and I worked two years before I came here. H'm! I guess you'll not work so long, Sugar Face! You'll get a feller and be married soon."

I looked at her. To work in that place for ten years, fifty-four hours a week, with only half an hour for lunch, inhale the dust from the wool, put a set of gold teeth in my mouth, and shrivel as she had — I thought, if I could not do better than that I would choose to die. But I had my hopes, my plans for the future — not the hope of getting married, but the hope of obtaining a profession, the hope of doing something worth while, hopes unexplainable, but so promising!

"No," I said, "I would never work so long."

She misunderstood me. "Oh, I kind o' thought so from the minute you came into the shop. Is not the foreman a nice feller, my Sugar Face?" she added ironically and walked away!

I had no time to pay attention to such remarks.

Nothing existed for me but the pursuits to which I gave my evenings. From my entrance into the shop in the morning, I waited for the clock to strike six, when I could leave the place and all in it behind me. Eating my dinner in a hurry, I would hasten to the Dramatic Club or some other place where I found companionship with people who had similar interests.

Five weeks passed, five happy weeks. I had already twenty-five dollars saved. My constant thought was, "I shall soon be able to buy a ticket and send for my brother."

But fate decided differently. On Monday of my sixth week, when I came into the shop the forelady came over to me and announced: "It has got slow, Sugar Face! there will be no work for you.—But what do you care for work?" she added laughingly.

She left me with no further explanation. I went over to the foreman to ask for a reason. He explained to me that it had turned slow and the boss kept only the quickest and cheapest hands, and the forelady was the one to select the fittest.

So I unexpectedly lost my job. What was I to do now?

With my lunch of two buttered rolls in my hands, I returned home.

New York with its slack season, New York and

starvation stared me in the face. But I refused to be discouraged. I had come to New York with eight dollars in my pocket. Now I had twenty-five. Am I not better off now? Did I not prepare myself to face the worst, to fight patiently? With a wealth of twenty-five dollars I should not starve. I quickly sat down to plan my expenditure, including my food allowance, for the following weeks.

Car fare	60 cents
Newspapers	6
Bread	25
Butter	20
Beans	14
Milk	20
Sugar	7
Total	$1.52

Plus $1.00 for room rent, $2.52 per week, subject to change as soon as I should find work.

The next thing was to decide what to look for. I knew no trade, and the season on sweaters would not begin for some time. I bought a paper and looked through the advertisements. It was too late to go out to look for a job that day, so I sat at home, reading.

My room-mate, a young Russian woman of twenty-five, worked on dresses at that time. She advised me to learn the dressmaking trade as the workers had begun to organize themselves seriously into a union and expected to better their conditions the coming season. Although living so close together, we had little in common. She was five years older than I and the hard life she led made her look sceptically at me and my optimistic views. Her husband in an insane asylum, her two children sent back to Russia to be in her old mother's care, she lived alone, separated from all her nearest and dearest. In her intense loneliness she sought forgetfulness in almost anything that would distract her thoughts and give her a passing pleasure. While I, young and ambitious, full of hope, was absorbed in different interests, and so our lives passed in different ways.

The next day I began to look for work. Day in, day out, I travelled the city from north to south, from east to west, in search of work. I answered all the advertisements, but in vain. I could find no job at dresses, because in the slack time no learners were taken. In general, learners found it hard to enter a trade. I tried straw hats, — the papers were full of advertisements for workers in that trade, — but I would have to pay twenty-five dollars and work for a month without pay in order to learn that trade. Flowers, corset-box making, everything I tried, and as the weeks passed, my courage lessened with each vanishing dollar.

And so more than a year had passed since I left home. Without English, with no relatives, I fought my battles bitterly. Now, on New Year's Eve, I had two dollars in my pocket, two dollars between me and starvation!

Tired, my head aching from the memories so vividly appearing before me, rushing so poignantly through my brain, I fell into restless sleep.

CHAPTER II

LATE the next morning, my room-mate woke me up.

"A friend is asking for you, Lisa," she said.

And in walked Clara with her familiar —

"Hello, kiddo! Get up quick, we must be at the club at eleven."

In a few minutes I was dressed and we went off. I could not understand what made her come for me. She had never visited me before.

"Are you out of work for a long time?" she asked as we walked together.

I told her all about my troubles, omitting to mention my two-dollar bill, all that was left to me for the indefinite future.

At the club the members were all there; those who were not acting were watching the others rehearse. Clara had the part of mother in the play being rehearsed. She usually played the mother's part in all the performances of the club and she was very good in her portrayals. Impatiently I waited until the rehearsal was over, when again Clara clung to me, insisting that I should go home and have dinner with her. I suspected that she might have guessed my situation and refused, but she insisted, so that, in the end, I went with her.

On the street she bought a newspaper, quickly opened it, glanced through it, and exclaimed delightedly: —

"Listen here — over fifty thousand girls in the ladies' garments trade, ready to walk out of the shops at the first call of their union, and strike for better conditions." She paused, then said: "I am ten years in the trade, and believe me, I had the time of my life working in those sweat-shops! For years we have tried to organize ourselves, but we were only a few in the field. It was hard to get the workers to understand the conditions in which they worked. Our last general strike that was called in 1909 was lost, and, mind you, the girls who worked in the worst sweat-shops did not go out; they were scabbing on us."

"What means a sweat-shop, Clara?" I interrupted her.

"Why, don't you know?" She looked at me in surprise. "The shops in which they work sometimes from fifty-six to sixty hours a week, in dark, dirty places, for terribly small wages, and treated awful! Those are the sweat-shops. Very often I used to be thrown out from shops just because I tried to agitate the girls against such conditions. And now, at last, we are getting them all, even the underwear and the kimono makers, those who were the worst-paid and worst-treated girls, often being compelled to pay for the use of the machines, pay for needles, electric power, and even for machine oil."

She went on telling of the struggles they had gone through; of the strikes; how the bosses hired gangsters to protect scabs; how she once caught a scab and, not being able to induce her to stop scabbing, beat her up so that she was afraid to go to work the next day.

"I assure you, I had not the heart to do it, but I could stand it no longer. We were striking for several weeks and many of our girls were nearly starved. Some were severely beaten up by the gangsters, and when that girl, after hearing our pleas, burst into laughter in our faces, I lost control. But I was so sorry afterwards that for days I walked around like one who had committed a crime," she concluded in her simple, frank, unpretentious language.

I studied her as she walked. Her face, bearing all the imprints of long, hard work, was in strong contrast to her heart, so childishly naïve, so enthusiastic, so full of life. Just for a bit of joy, she was ready to forgive the world all the wrongs it had done to her.

The club was her only solace. A child of poor Galicia, having hardly any education, working since she was ten years old, she zealously strove for education in the evenings. Soul-hunger for beauty, for art, for good literature, brought her to the club, to which she willingly gave her time and her money that she might help to keep it up, to build a temple of art which might help educate those who were so brutally deprived of education, as she had been. It was in that work that she found expression for her beautiful desires and rest from the monotonous prosaic life she lived amid the sordid surroundings of the crowded East Side. My admiration for her grew more and more as we continued to walk.

Into a dark hall on Avenue B Clara led me. On the third floor we stopped. The door was opened to us by Clara's mother, a tired-out, elderly woman of fifty. She seemed to have expected me, for the table was set for two, and the rest of the family, having had their dinner, were all gone.

From the attention paid to me by Clara's mother, I understood that Clara must have spoken to her about me. The thought that Clara might have invited me, suspecting that I was in need, insulted me. I sat awkwardly at the table and choked with each mouthful of food.

"Try this little cake, you will surely like it. Take this too: it's all home-made," her mother kept on, insisting on helping me to the various delicious cakes. "Home-made" echoed painfully in my ears. I had not had a real home-made meal for so many days. Those home-made meals I used to get in a private family when I had money to pay for them were only "made" for the money I paid.

The meal prepared by a mother to suit the tastes of her children, I had so longed for. It was the mother's touch that was lacking in the boarding-house meals.

I watched Clara. She certainly had a good appetite and consumed one thing after another, not fearing that the "mistress" will, perhaps, watch her, thinking that she eats more than her board-money pays for.

"Are you not happy to have your mother and folks with you? It must be wonderful to be together!" I exclaimed longingly.

"I should say so," Clara answered self-contentedly. And then, looking up at her mother, her face suddenly changed its expression and she turned her head away and heaved a great sigh, much to my amazement.

After dinner we went into the parlor, furnished with some second-hand chairs, a few art postals on the walls, and some cheap statuettes of Beethoven and Mozart on the imitation marble mantelpiece.

Our conversation again turned on the coming strike.

"I think that the best plan for you is to learn the dressmaking. True, it will take you some time and you cannot make much money while learning, but you will, at least, have a trade in the end. Without a trade you will very often not find work even in the busiest season."

I agreed with her, but how was I to find a place to learn?

"Now, let's see — Mr. N." — she mentioned the name of a member of our club — "keeps a small dress-shop and I am sure that he'll take you in when I speak to him."

"Is he really a manufacturer?" I exclaimed, a ray of hope creeping into my heart. "Why, I am sure that he will take me in!"

I was a little surprised to have a real "boss" a member of our club.

The very same evening we spoke to Mr. N. and, oh, wonder of wonders, he told me to come the next morning.

At six o'clock I was up, impatiently waiting for the clock to strike eight.

At the door of the shop I met a gentleman, somewhat resembling my Mr. N., but older, who asked me whom I wished to see.

"I am to see Mr. N. He told me to come this morning. He — he — wants — to give — me a job — on dresses."

I trembled, discouraged by his surprised, displeased look.

"You mean my brother. Well, I don't think we need any help; the season has not yet begun."

Like one who had suddenly had cold water poured over her, I was chilled by his last words.

"You see, Mr. N., I am only to learn the trade, so that it does not matter whether it is busy or not. I may learn something till the season starts and be able to earn some money then."

My appealing voice must have impressed him. He opened the door and told me to come in and wait for his brother. It was a very light, clean, little shop, with two rows of tables, — ten machines on each one, — one long cutting-table, and one table with a pressing-board.

A little after eight two girls with dark complexions walked in and, looking at me with curiosity, they turned to Mr. N. questioningly. The latter told them that I was waiting for his brother.

At half-past eight, that half-hour stretching like a century, the younger Mr. N. came in. Greeting me familiarly, he introduced me to his brother and the two girls, who were his sisters, and who already sat at their machines, increasing their speed by singing a merry Russian song.

"We are here our own family. There are two more of our intimate friends working with us, two Italian finishers, and one presser — that is our staff. I do the cutting, my brother the designing, and so we are all working hard for our living," Mr. N. concluded smilingly; and bringing a bundle to me, he asked his sister to instruct me.

"Do you speak Russian?" she inquired as she bent over me to show me what to do.

"Why, yes," I answered.

"Oh, is that so!" she said, pleased with my answer and began in a fluent but ungrammatical Russian to cross-question me: Where did I come from? What did I do? How did I like this and that? — never giving me a chance to answer any of her questions. She told me all she could about herself, chattering all day without stopping. About the work she would speak with high authority, assuring me that it would take me months to become a skilled worker.

"Do you know, Louis, this little girl speaks Russian?" she said to the older brother.

"Does she?" he answered, looking at me approvingly and coming over to our table. He seemed to regard me with more respect for knowing Russian.

"I am going to the opera to-night," my instructor announced, ripping apart the yoke of a waist that I tried to make into a collar.

"You do not even ask me with whom I am going?" she continued, not getting any reply from me. "My gentleman friend is a musician, you know, and we often go to the opera. Do you like music?"

"Very much," I replied, trying to discourage conversation, for she gave me very little chance to work.

"What about your gentleman friend? You surely have one — is he musical?"

Heavens! Will she never stop? I wondered.

"You do like to know a lot of things all in one day," I replied. I spoke softly so as not to displease her, but she went over to her machine and spoke to me no more that day.

On the eleventh day of my apprenticeship the long-expected strike broke out. The very small staff in our shop, being so closely related to the boss, did not stop work. My employer tried to convince me that it would be very foolish of me to join the strikers when I was only a stranger in the trade.

I did not know what to do. Indeed, I knew very little about the American Labor Movement in general and less about that particular industry. Should the employees in my shop walk out, there would be no doubts for me, but they did not. Being in the first stage of apprenticeship, not knowing the people nor the real conditions existing in the trade, I thought that I could be of no help to the strikers, so stayed in the shop and learned the work. I could not make up a garment, nor even, as yet, had I succeeded in making a straight stitch. Still, each bundle that went through my hands caused me terrible sufferings. It seemed as if the goods would look up at me reproachfully. "So many young girls fighting for a better chance, for more freedom, for a better life! Leave us untouched in the baskets."

"But I am not injuring them, I am only learning," I tried to quiet my conscience. "I am learning in order to help them when I have a right to stand in their ranks and demand the same: to fight for a better life, for freedom."

Oh! that better life! Who more than I had struggled for it?

Who more than I had sacrificed for freedom — a freedom that I have not yet realized?

In the evenings, when I walked home, I tried to slip through the pickets so they should not notice me; for they would not believe that I was only a learner and that my heart and soul were with them.

With delight and envy I watched those young, brave children in the picket line, not fearing the policemen who would chase them from one place to another, nor the gangsters hired by the bosses, who would stain with blood many a young girl's face when she dared to speak to a scab who was under their protection.

The first weeks of my apprenticeship did not go at all smoothly. My employer friend seemed to grow discouraged with me because I still did not seem to distinguish a sleeve from a front or a back from a yoke.

My talkative instructor would cry out in disgust: "You certainly botch up all the work! If you go on this way, you will earn enough for water, but not for bread."

Crowning me with a nickname, the first day, she would often tease me to tears. As she was known as the "gypsy," she called me "the little white angel," for my small stature and my white complexion. Seeing how little I liked that name, even the beautiful Italians teased me good-naturedly.

One evening the elder Mr. N. called me over, and in a friendly manner advised me to give up the job. He said I was an intelligent girl and could never concentrate my mind on the machine enough to become a real worker and earn my living by it.

Another blow to my hopes. Did he really mean it?

"Perhaps he is right. I shall never be able to learn a trade if I progress so slowly," I thought. "Perhaps I am too old to learn anything at all. I am already passed twenty and am still helpless as a child."

He seemed to notice my depression, for he immediately changed his mind, and accompanying me home that evening he talked to me for a long time.

After he left me, I went down-hearted to my room. "What shall I do? How much more must I concentrate my mind on the machine? Am I not trying hard to learn? Why does it seem to go so slow?"

The other girls are so quick, everything from their hands comes out so smoothly, and when I try to do the same thing, I start so fine, but it comes out so crooked! How shall I learn? How shall I learn? That question kept digging, digging in my mind, filling me with despair.

I thought of my older boss.

He was so kind to me, he spoke so nicely, with more sympathy than any one else had done since I left home. No one till then had inquired how I was living, not even my room-mate knew how I made ends meet.

To my parents I had to lie. Each letter I wrote to them made them think that I was quite contented with the new life. The thought that they might learn the truth made me so miserable, so miserable. Had they not objected to my leaving home?

I was to be strong, I was to overcome everything. But how, how? I feared that I was too weak, too helpless against life. I saw no hope of earning enough money to help my family as I had promised. I saw no possibility of studying in the evenings when my mind was so worried about my daily bread. If I cannot accomplish anything, what is life for, then? Lying in bed that night I began to think of suicide.

Oh, how I wished to die that evening, to be relieved from the eternal anxiety, from painful disappointments!

"But suicide is a selfish thing," I thought. "If I find relief in that, what about those who survive? Will not the deed kill my parents, who have so much faith in my strength? No, I shall not disappoint them; I shall fight until I succeed. Others struggle as much as I do. I have heard of so many who have suffered as much and more than I and yet were successful in the end. Why should not I? I shall prove my ambitions. I must."

With a terrible headache, I fell into an unsound sleep, my head whirling into a heavy nightmare.

In my dreams I wandered aimlessly — now climbing up muddy hills and falling back from the heights — now fluttering over cities, deserted streets, and dark harbors. Then I dropped on a dock, painfully watching a ship sailing — something was in it that I feared to lose with its disappearance. A tall figure in white appeared before me. It stretched its hand toward the sea and the sailing ship.

"The sea is your life," it said. "In that ship is hidden your future, your success. If you are strong, if you have courage, go swim after it, reach it, and you will conquer; happiness will be yours."

With the last words it faded in the thick fog, while I was thrown into the sea. With my hands I began to break through the muddy waves. My struggle had no end. Many, many days I swam, but the faster I swam, the more quickly the ship seemed to recede from me. My strength gradually lessened. I grew more tired. I rallied and made great efforts to swim faster. Little by little the water began to dry out. The ship disappeared from my sight, and soon I found myself in a swamp.

I was beginning to sink — another instant and I was swallowed in the mud. "Help! Help!" I cried out, and awoke.

It was early morning. I jumped up, dressed quickly and went out to breathe a little fresh air, still tired and under the spell of the night's terrible dream.

Why was it so terrible, after all? I did not believe in dreams, but that dream seemed to have symbolized my life's struggle.

On a bench in Union Square I sat waiting for the clock to strike eight, for our shop never opened before that hour. Thousands of people passed the square, most of them garment-workers.

So many people could learn the trade. Why not I? "I shall learn it under any circumstances, and that quickly, too," I decided.

I reached the shop, just as my boss who had accompanied me home the night before unlocked the door.

"Good-morning; who threw you out of bed so early?" he said, and added smilingly, "Now we shall see what we can do for you, little angel."

"Oh, please, Mr. N., you, too! You must excuse me, if I ask you not to call me a nickname. I am already twenty years old and I think I am too old to be teased," I said.

He apologized. "Why, I did not think that you would feel badly about it. Goodness! You do not look twenty, at all. I thought you were not more than sixteen or seventeen."

His sisters came in, the power opened, and we sat down to work. During the next few days I exerted myself to the utmost. My boss helped me, and as my work went on improving, I began to feel more at my ease. Another two weeks and no more botching; I was able to put a garment together, but I was still very slow and the prices were poor. I could make only from five to six dollars a week. That money was just enough to live from hand to mouth, and I needed so many things. My shoes were worn out; my clothes, too, were shabby; I had nothing but the dress I had on.

Meantime the strike of the garment-workers was settled. The workers returned to their shops with great victory, their union recognized, their prices almost doubled, their hours reduced from fifty-four to fifty a week. We still worked under the old conditions. Our boss claimed that he could not raise the prices because his concern was small, and could not turn out much work. I was so much obliged to him for the favor he had done to me that I felt that I had no right to contradict or be displeased; but as I was unable to better my scanty living from my small means, I began to grow discouraged again.

My idea of studying in the evenings had to be given up for the present, because I worked too hard all day, and in the evenings I had to do my washing and mending and prepare my breakfast and lunch for the next day, since I could not afford to get my meals outside.

"Heavens! Where is my freedom? I work in the shop by day; I also work in the evenings; no time for anything else but work and eat. This is not a very interesting life. What will the outcome be?"

There was something else to worry me. My boss's kindness to me created such a warm gratitude in me toward him. Being very romantic, and foolishly naïve, I took my feelings for him too seriously and began to fear that I might fall in love with him. I had heard of so many cases of employees who fell in love with their employers and the sad results that followed.

But I wanted to lead my life in purity. I did not want any one to soil my path. I feared that if life continued as it was, I might be plunged into the dirty slough as many others were, and I decided to prefer death if it came, rather than allow anything to happen to me.

One evening, coming home from work, so tired and discouraged, I found a letter from home with very sad news. My family was in hardship, and though they did not ask me for anything, I knew that if I could send them money it would be of great help to them.

What was I to do? I hardly had enough for my board, but they knew nothing of my circumstances, and never would I want them to know. When would I be able to help them? My father, deprived of my help, had to hire some one in my place, besides paying the chief of police and keeping up such a large family.

"Oh! when will it end, when will it end? If I only had the money! Money! Money! How hateful you are, but, oh, how I need to have you!"

Enfolded in the dark clouds that again spread over my horizon, I began to lose ground. My head burning, my thoughts in confusion, I ran down the stairs to the street and carelessly wandered among the crowded pushcarts.

"A penny! A penny a sweet potato! A penny a pickle! All your heart's desire, only one penny!" rang the loud voices of the peddlers.

Sweet potatoes, pickles, bananas on the pushcarts, a skirt, a waist, a front, a yoke in the basket at the side of my machine, the letter from home, money — my boss — all danced before my eyes, in dark confusion.

Flowers! I stopped near a flower store, attracted

by the American Beauties in the windows. Unthinkingly I walked in.

"Well, madam, birthday, wedding, funeral bouquets, — what do you desire?"

"Birthday, wedding, funeral bouquets," I repeated absent-mindedly.

"Funeral bouquet," I said.

"How much?"

"How much?" I repeated. "Just a second." I began to count my change — a dollar, twenty-five, forty-five, sixty-nine cents. "For a dollar sixty-nine cents, please."

I remember the man looked at me in amazement.

"Madame, we do not sell for a dollar sixty-nine cents — a dollar fifty, if you please."

"Let it be a dollar fifty," I said carelessly.

With the bouquet in my hands I walked home. My room-mate was away in the picketing line — her shop was still on strike. I did not expect her until late in the evening. I had plenty of time —

The flowers, the beautiful white roses, the lilies — ah, the odor intoxicated me. Why did I not get an American Beauty, that I am so fond of?

An American Beauty in a funeral bouquet?

Oh, yes, a funeral — death — suicide — my home — my people —

Slowly I turned on the gas, and made a solution of poisonous matches.

My room-mate returned unexpectedly. I sent her out, and quickly drank the solution —

I recovered consciousness in the hospital, doctors and nurses around me. Unfortunately, the matches were not poisonous and I was brought back to life. The next day Clara and my room-mate were with me — Clara, her eyes filled with tears.

"You foolish child, to do such a silly thing!"

I spoke to neither of them. I was so tired. I wanted to be quiet, to have nobody around me, to be left alone to my own thoughts.

CHAPTER III

AFTER four days in the hospital, I was well enough to come out.

"Will you not come to us, where mother will take good care of you for a time?" Clara begged me.

I refused. I wanted to be no burden to anybody. She brought her mother to the hospital and, both insisting, I at last consented. Where else was I to go, my last cent spent for the flowers?

Under her mother's watchful care I soon began to feel better and wanted to go to work, but they would not hear of it, until I was completely rested.

My thought that Clara was very fortunate in having her family with her proved unfounded. She had four younger sisters and two brothers. Her father had died when she was only ten years of age, and as the oldest in the family she was the first to be sent to work. She was apprenticed to a tailor, but he, instead of teaching her the trade, used her as his messenger and oftener as nurse to his babies. Very often the ten-year-old wage-earner would forget her duties and stop on the street to play with children of her own age; then her employer would scold her for still having those "childish nonsenses in her head."

At sixteen she came to America. As a skilled

dressmaker she easily found work, but was never paid her worth. For seven or eight dollars a week she worked from seven in the morning until eight or nine in the evening.

Living on three dollars a week, doing her own washing and ironing and mending, she saved the rest of the money in order to bring her people over here. When, at last, she succeeded in bringing them over, and had furnished an apartment and helped each one of them to become self-supporting, they gave her little appreciation for all she had suffered for them. The two brothers left the home to seek their fortunes all for themselves. The older sisters went to work. The younger ones went to school and through Clara's efforts enjoyed a few years of education, but when, at last, they were able to support themselves their respect for her was gone. They would make fun of her incorrect English, make light of her ideals, and her devotion to the club. Having profited by her sacrifices and gained through her what she had coveted for herself but had never been able to obtain, — an education, — they looked down on her because she had not their superficial knowledge of American customs, language, and cheap styles. They deemed that she lacked culture and refinement because in the public schools they had received false ideas of externals. Their understanding of Americanism was limited to speaking English, wearing high pompadours and powdering their noses. Clara, with her delightful simplicity, her love of real beauty, her great big sympathetic heart, so ready to help every one who appealed to her, was ignored and trampled on, her life embittered by the sisters for whom she had made her greatest sacrifices.

The poor, hard-working mother suffered from the ingratitude of the younger daughters and was powerless to help it. They would not listen to her; they failed to realize that her heart was bleeding, her hair turning white from grief.

After two weeks I was strong enough to go to work. As I did not want work with my former employer, I did not return there, but went with one of Clara's friends, a cutter, to the place where he was employed. It was also a non-union shop, one of quite a number — almost a hundred — that remained unorganized, the workers trusting their bosses' promise to better conditions without the help of the union. Like sheep led by wolves, who try to make the sheep believe that the shepherd is their enemy because he does not allow them to run freely over the spacious fields and gather of the best grass, and that without the shepherd they would enjoy more freedom. The foolish sheep influenced by the wolves run away from the shepherd only to be all eaten up by the hungry wolves who had purposely led them away from protection.

It was the height of the season. Labor was

scarce, and the boss was obliged to grant the best union conditions in order to prevent his workers from leaving. The system was very different from that of my first place. (Later I learned that each shop has its own system.) I felt like a beginner again.

The forelady, Yetta, — bless her heart! — was a kind, gentle person. She gave me all the necessary instructions so that I soon overcame my difficulties. Week-work prevailed in the place. I expected to get seven dollars a week to start with, and great was my astonishment when in my first pay envelope I found ten dollars. Destiny seemed to play with me. I was so happy that evening when I brought my pay home! Breathless, I ran to Clara and, holding the envelope tight in my hand, before her eyes, I asked her to guess how much. She could not guess. The highest she could think of was eight, but when I showed her the envelope she shouted with joy.

"Here! Here! you are a regular dressmaker already!"

"Why, how dare you think otherwise?" I answered in a teasing tone.

It was not the money that made me feel so happy, it was my worth that I thought of. I could not have expected to get ten dollars a week after having only a few weeks of experience. My former boss, when I made five dollars a week, liked to remind me that he did not think that I was worth even that much. Though claiming to be my friend, he took advantage of a learner, as nearly every other manufacturer does.

Now that I was able to make ends meet more easily, my mind was at peace again. I began to think of my home and decided to send for my younger brother, a strongly built lad, now about eighteen. He, I thought, having a good trade, will soon be able to earn money and both of us will help the rest of the family. Here again my friend Clara helped me — she gave me a loan of fifty dollars on payments of three dollars a week. The money I sent home for my brother's ticket. I went on improving in my work and soon I was sent occasionally to the sample-room, and so became a sample-maker.

Things once more went on smoothly. The strength of youth conquered and my cheerfulness returned. Again, I went singing among my friends, infecting them with my joyousness. Even in the shop I was happy. My neighbors were very kind. Each one would help the other out of difficulties in the work.

At lunch-time very few of us would go out. We ate together. Bologna sausages, corned beef, the Italians' eggplant fried in olive oil — all spread a mixed, unpleasant smell over the shop. The few girls at my table would exchange food with each other, a cherry chocolate for an orange, a piece of apple for a banana, a corned-beef sandwich for some white fish. I would take part in the conversation, but never shared in the exchange of food. Their kind offerings to me I refused also, for I had nothing to give in return. My lunch consisted of either a cheese sandwich and milk or an egg and milk. The pint of milk I bought every morning for my breakfast had to be used up, so I had a small bottle and would always bring the rest of it for my lunch.

"No wonder you are so white — living on nothing but milk," they would often tease me.

I told them I liked nothing else, though often their pickles and smoked fish would awaken a sharp appetite in me.

Their conversation, so different from the vulgarities of the girls in the sweater shop, was much pleasanter. There was little talk here about the "fellers," "swell" evening pumps, and lace petticoats that the six-dollar wage-earners in the sweater shop were constantly discussing. Here we talked about questions of the day, world happenings, music, art, literature, and trade questions. One fault I found with them: their indifference to being members of the Waist and Dressmakers' Union. They would belong, — they all agreed, — if they worked in a union shop, but they would not trouble to unionize this shop.

Although the conditions in my shop were just as good as in the best union shops, — we had everything except the recognition of the union, — still, I was anxious to have it organized. I confess it was puzzling to me at first to understand why the boss objected to his people joining the union. As long as union conditions prevailed in the shop, why not allow the workers to belong where they ought to belong? Some of the workers in the shop were union members. On my question, Why did they not have the shop organized? they would answer me carelessly, "We should worry so long as we have union conditions." I suffered by their ignorant answers. I recalled the thousands of young girls who had so bitterly fought their fight only a few weeks before, and I argued with my co-workers.

"Don't you know that we have got everything just because so many thousands of girls fought for it? You yourselves admit that the standards here were much lower before the general strike was called. You only got increases when the girls in the other shops won them. Do you think that our boss, no matter how kind he is, would reduce four hours a week if it were not for the strike? We workers must all do our share. It is not fair to stand aside and let others fight and spend their money to keep up an organization when we all get the benefits from it.

"There must be reasons why the boss does not

want a union shop. I am not criticizing our boss. I admit that he is a fair man. But don't you know that for the sake of being successful in business, of making more money, the bosses, even the best of them, will exploit their workers to the utmost? That is why we must be organized so that we can stand up against them. In unity is our strength. We must belong to a union in order to protect ourselves against the ruling hand of capitalism."

But the workers cared to know next to nothing about it. Some of the girls would answer me rudely: —

"You had better shut up; if you don't you will get fired. There was another girl in the shop who tried to agitate for the union and she was discharged."

I would often talk to Clara about my desire to organize the shop. She also warned me not to do it. "The dull season is approaching, and you have not any money saved to face it, so what will you do in case you are fired?"

But I could not rest. I felt like a criminal to work in a trade that is organized and not belong to the ranks. I could not imagine that there were workers who as yet did not understand the value of organization.

But I soon found the reason for such ignorance. As a rule the worker in a shop brings to it his or her friend or relative; that friend or relative brings another friend, so that in most cases, each shop contains workers who are closely related to each other. The consequence is that if one seems to be misinformed about unionism, all of them get the same idea. If one of them is warned by the boss to keep away from union people, most all of them obey him.

Particularly among Italians the bringing in of friends is practiced. Very often you see in a shop a set of finishers who are nearly all Italians. There are mothers and mothers-in-law, daughters and daughters-in-law, sisters, and so on. If you can persuade one to join the union, you may be sure of getting them all; if you fail with one, you fail with all. It was so with our shop. All the finishers and cleaners were Italians; the drapers, Yiddish and Italians; the examiners were Americans, who considered it beneath their dignity to belong to a "labor organization," especially to a "Yiddish Union" as they called the Waist and Dressmakers' Union. The operators were mixed — mostly Jews, Italians, and a few Americans. As a matter of fact, they were all related, — the Jews to Jews, the Italians to their people, — and if some were misinformed about the union, the rest were, also, and hated to be agitated about it.

Realizing that, lacking knowledge of the trade-union movement, I could do very little, I decided to report to the union, hoping that it would help me to organize my shop.

When I went to the office of the union and asked for the organizer and told him what I wanted, he appreciated my efforts and explained that the organizers were only too glad to help out those who wanted to be helped. They had been trying for years to enlighten the workers' minds, to awaken them to self-consciousness, and to help them organize into unions.

"Without a union," he said, "the bosses drive their workers like slaves; they do not fear the individual. If any one protests, he or she is promptly thrown out of the shop, but when a protest comes from all the workers, not only from one shop, but from all shops equally, the bosses must listen and treat the matter justly; if they do not, then the workers strike. It is very sad to admit that there are still workers who do not care how they are treated. Instead of demanding their rights, they are constantly trying schemes to win the bosses' favor in order to get a raise of one dollar."

He spoke the truth, — there are many workers who would do anything, even injure a fellow-worker, in order to get a raise.

Somehow my boss learned that I had been to the union. Any one else in my place would have been "fired" without any explanation, but I worked for ten dollars a week and worked mostly on samples, while a sample-maker usually gets fourteen dollars. That is why the boss first tried to warn me.

In the morning, when I came to work, the designer, a very gentle woman, always welcoming me with a smile, seemed to be angry.

"Why, Lizzie, I am surprised at you, — such a sensible girl as I thought you, — to act so silly."

I guessed what she meant, but asked, "What is the matter?" as if I had not understood.

"Tell me, are you dissatisfied with your position? Is there anything wrong with this place?"

"No," I answered; "I'm satisfied, and I think the place is all right."

"Then what is the sense in going to that damn union?"

"'Damn union'! How dare you?" I wanted to reply, but I controlled myself.

"Well," I said, "I see no harm in it."

"It is for your sake I warn you. I'm only a friend to you. Don't you know that the leaders of the union only care for your money? They are not doing a thing for you. They are grafters; that is all they are."

I smiled again. Poor soul! She was so sure of what she said.

Soon the boss came in and called me aside. With the authority of a professor, he began to lecture me.

"Look here, little girl, I'm a man who is as fair and square as possible. I always treat my workers as good as I can. Everybody is pleased with their positions; are not you? Did I not try to give you all chances for advancement?"

"Yes, you did, and it was very nice of you, but you did not raise me in accordance with my advancement," I answered.

"Oh, you'll get a raise next season. You don't expect me to raise you the first season. But, to the point. You have no idea what grafters the labor leaders are. There has been no strike which has not been sold by them. They get the poor working-people's money and use it for their own benefit. Now, I am sorry for my own people. Why should they waste their money earned through hard labor? The union is only a bluff; there is nothing to it; it is not good for the workers. Now, if you want to be a sensible girl, do your work and do not mix in other people's business. You can stay here, and I'll raise you a dollar on the week when the next season begins. Now I can't. You see the dull season is coming already. Another week and there will be very little work to do."

I thanked him for his kindness and sat down to work. Now I understood why people in that shop feared the union. They were fed with the same kind of lectures continuously. No wonder they had an idea of unions in general as organizations where the workers were cheated. How was I to change their minds? How was I to explain to them that this was only a trick to poison the workers' minds?

Later, when I worked in other shops, I heard similar stories told to the workers by the bosses.

In order to learn what our unions are and help organize the workers, I joined the union. I began at once to look up the reports so as to find out how the general strike had been settled, and to learn the history of the development of our union. Since the year 1900, the union, consisting then of very few members, had tried earnestly to organize the workers and to uplift the trade. The strikes that had been called had never been very successful because only a minority of the workers were members of the union. The heroic struggle of the few resulted in long weeks of starvation among the strikers, broken heads, arrests of pickets, and workhouse sentences for the young girls who tried to better their working conditions rather than to turn for their living to the "paths of shame."

For years these few heroic, intelligent workers had fearlessly carried on the agitation for conditions that would make possible a more human life among their ranks, until at last, in 1912, the big mass of down-trodden workers raised their heads, responded to the call, and began preparations for a big demonstration during the coming year.

The Manufacturers' Association in the dress and waist industry controlled nearly two thirds of the trade. The association realized the widespread agitation and foresaw the strike as the result of the growing strength of the union. Having the benefit of the experience of the cloak industry, which had adopted a protocol agreement in 1910, the association had begun, as early as November, to confer with the Waist and Dressmakers' Union, wishing to adopt an agreement that would prevent strikes in future. On January 18, 1913, a protocol agreement was consummated between the Manufacturers' Association and the union. It aimed to enlist both parties in an effort to improve conditions and to obtain the equalization of standards throughout the industry by peaceful and honorable means. It was agreed to create a joint board of sanitary control to insure sanitary conditions in the factory — sufficient light and ventilation, safety, and freedom from fire and overcrowding. A board of grievances was also created, consisting of ten members, five representing the union and five the manufacturers, to adjust all disputes and settle controversies; and a board of arbitration to decide all disputes that the board of grievances were unable to settle. No strike or lockout was to take place until these two boards had had the opportunity to try to adjust matters between the disputants.

A wage scale board was provided on which likewise both the manufacturers and the union were represented, to standardize the prices to be paid for piece- and week-work. The board was to reserve data and statistics with the hope of establishing a scientific basis for the fixing of prices of week- and piece-work throughout the industry that would insure a minimum wage and at the same time permit reward for increased efficiency. The board was empowered to make an immediate and thorough investigation into the existing rates paid for labor, the earnings of the operatives, and the classification of garments in the industry. Sub-contracting was to be abolished.

The term "sub-contracting" is used when one skilled worker in a shop has under his control from one to ten unskilled workers; he is responsible for the work and is paid for it, paying to his helpers what he deems necessary. Sub-contracting is very ruinous to the workers. The sub-contractors naturally try to make as much as they can from the workers, and the labor of a garment is extensively subdivided, each worker in the set receiving only one part of the garment. As he quickly specializes, working on that part exclusively, he increases his speed. But the subdivision of the work gives no chance to the workers to learn the whole trade sufficiently to better themselves; thus, as learners, they are always dependent on the man for whom they work, receiving from him from three to six dollars a week. The speed with which he drives them to work injures their health, and they are also the cause of lowering the prices for the skilled workers.

A minimum wage for week-workers was fixed.

Operators were to be paid by the piece. They were given an increase, so that no average operator would earn less than thirty cents an hour on piece-work. The standard price per hour was to be finally fixed, after investigation by the board, within the following six months.

Besides the Manufacturers' Association there were a number of manufacturers who did not belong to the association and they signed individual agreements with the union. They were called the "Independent Union Shops."

I was very much inspired when I finished reading the "Protocol of Peace." It seemed as if everything was accomplished. The workers had at last compelled the manufacturers to recognize their rights. Each paragraph read: — "Both parties agree"; "Both parties are desirous —"

I thought the workers in the union shops must be happy, for they seemed to have everything to protect them, and I wished so much to work in a union shop. But I soon learned that it was not so, that so-called "industrial democracy" existed only within the pages of the "Protocol of Peace."

The third week in April work began to slacken. In the shops where a high grade of dresses is made, the season often ends that month. On the coming Saturday, at one o'clock, the boss in my shop informed his workers that on account of the approaching dull season he was compelled to reduce their wages from two to three dollars a week, demanding, however, the same full week's work of labor.

What were the workers to do? Here they were like sheep led away by the wolf from the shepherd. They had listened to the boss when he promised them all they desired, in order to keep them from the union, and now, when the busy season was over, he took advantage of the workers who had no union to protect them and reduced their wages, being sure that in the dull season they would stay for less money.

Did the workers at last realize it? Some did, and left the place; those who remained were too ignorant to realize it.

When I came on Monday to work, everything seemed so different. No more the former gentleness; the foreman was more particular about the work, more exacting in his demands. As there was less to do, he had more time to watch everything. Even the nice Yetta was not so gentle, but I knew it was not her fault. She had to obey the instructions of the boss.

The first of May was approaching; the union made all preparations for a grand parade.

The first of May had two meanings for me. As school-teacher at home, I always celebrated that day by going off with my pupils to the woods, where we spent a merry holiday in songs and games. Sweet were my memories of those bygone May days.

The second and more important meaning was the "International Labor Holiday." Internationalism appealed to me greatly and I decided to stop from work even if the boss should be against it. In vain did I try to inspire my co-workers with the significance of the first of May. They refused to give up a day's wages for such a sentimentality.

The day fell on Thursday, a bright, warm spring day. Many thousands of young girls, in uniforms of white waists with red collars, formed in line, ready to march. The sun illuminated their pale but happy faces. As they walked through the avenues and streets, looking up at the sky-scrapers where they slaved all the year, their eyes would shine with pride and hope. They looked as if they would speak and warn the world: "Behold, you who keep us in the darkness, no more are we to slave for you. Together we stand now, — men and women, creators of wealth, — and together we shall stand to fight for our rights!"

I kept my holiday, marching with a small separate division of girls who gathered from different non-union shops and, like myself, perhaps risked their jobs for observing the holiday. The rest of the day I spent happily with my friends. But I paid for that day with many, many miserable weeks.

CHAPTER IV

THE sun's rays, creeping into my tiny room on the top floor, joyfully played on my face when I awoke early the next morning. I lay in bed leisurely stretching and relaxing my poor legs, tired from marching. I was still full of the events of yesterday. My heart beat with warmth as I lay enjoying my sun bath. The clock struck seven, time to get ready for work. Humming a favorite Malo-Russian folk-song I quickly dressed, took my usual breakfast, — a roll and a cup of milk, — which tasted so good that day, and went down to the shop. It was a glorious morning. The little buds on the trees in Madison Square were just opening into beautiful bloom and spread a pleasant fragrance around. The small fountain in the centre bubbled, bubbled, splashing out right and left. I stooped for a moment to enjoy the cold sprinkles on my face.

The great mass of workers who were passing by all seemed so light-hearted. It was the beautiful morning, the warm sun, the awakening of the green, that spread the good-humor on their faces.

I liked all the world, and in my heart greeted everybody and everything.

"Good-morning!" — "Good-morning!" "A fine morning!" "A glorious morning!" "Well — how did you like the march? Was it not splendid?" "Indeed, it was wonderful!" was heard all around as the workers met on their way to the shops.

"Good-morning," said I merrily to the foreman, who happened to be the first to meet me when I entered the shop.

"Good-morning," came an angry nasal sound.

"It is too nice a morning to be angry," I teased.

"If you think that you can make a living on nice mornings or May holidays, you need not come in to work!" he answered severely.

I understood that something was wrong and that my good-humor would not gain the foreman's favor, so I quietly went to my machine and bent my head over my work.

Meantime, the girls began to fill up their places at the machines. Some would stop near me while passing and question how the march looked.

"I paid with a day's wages to know, and I think that it is too expensive to tell," was my reply to all of them.

"Good-morning, Miss Union lady!" I jumped up, instinctively feeling that it was I who was addressed.

A sudden laughter rang over the shop from the amused workers.

On the other side of the table stood the boss,

calling me angrily. With a sudden foreboding of evil, I walked over to him.

"Look here, miss, you know that I think that you are too smart for my place."

"What is it?" I interrupted.

"What it is? Just as if you did not know! I don't want you to make trouble in my shop. What business have you to bother my workers? You made some of them stop from work when I was in a rush to finish out a lot of dresses."

"Why, you complain all the time that there is nothing to do and your workers sit idle. How did you happen to have such a rush all of a sudden?"

"Oh, you get on my nerves! You seem to know everything that is not your business! I am not going to stand it any longer!" he said disgustedly, and walked away.

On Saturday I received my pay and was discharged. And so I lost my job for celebrating the first of May.

Now that I had to look for another job, I made up my mind to get a place in a union shop. I hoped that in the union shops the bosses carried out the agreements of the protocol, but I soon found out that the workers had to fight for every bit that the agreements were supposed to bring them.

The dull season had already begun and it was not easy to find a job. In the shops where a cheap line of dresses or waists is made, the busy season lasts until July. So I hoped to get work in some of these places. I had worked on a good line of dresses that require more skill and care, and could expect to earn but very little on the cheaper grades where speed was required more than skill.

I was told that I must go out very early in order to get a job, for there were many other girls who were also looking for work. So on Monday morning I took a paper and went out. There were many advertisements for operators. As I was accustomed to work on samples, I could do everything on a garment, — operating, draping, examining, and finishing. I ran over the lines again and again, trying to find from the advertisements which were union shops and which was the best, but the lines told me nothing. So I just went to the nearest place. When I arrived, a score of girls were already standing by the door waiting for the employer. They did not look very friendly at each other: each one fearing in the other her competitor. We waited for a long time, until, at last, His Majesty the Employer came out, a very unsympathetic-looking fellow with a long curved nose and still more unattractive voice.

"Vot you vant, girls?" he asked in dry broken English.

The girls rushed over to him. "You advertised for operators." "I am an experienced operator." All of them began to talk at once.

"Joos a moment, joos a moment! Don't rush! I send the foreman out to you."

We waited a long time until the foreman came out. A young, neat-looking man, he seemed more friendly to us.

"What is it you want, girls?" — the same question as the boss.

"You want operators, don't you?" the girls all questioned in reply.

"Let's see, what can you do?" He took each one separately and cross-examined her, and then, when he had finished with all of us, he said, "I need only two." The rest had to go.

I felt hurt, not because I did not get the position, but because I felt it was unfair to keep all the girls waiting for more than an hour when he needed only two. As it was after nine o'clock I thought it was too late to look for another job that day, so I went home. I had only twelve dollars in my possession. Six dollars rent for my little sunny room on the top floor would leave me only six. That amount could not carry me very far.

The next morning I went again, but I did not go before eight o'clock. I did not want to stand with so many other job-seekers, for I could not push them away and rush to the boss as some of them did. I tried my luck at nine o'clock when everybody either had a place or had gone home. I found a place as an operator on West 25th Street, a union shop.

I did more observing than sewing that first day. I had never worked in a union shop before, and I was anxious to find out how the people feel there, how the organized workers behave toward one another. I knew that in a non-union shop the workers have very little to say about their conditions. The employer fixes the prices, discharges a worker whenever he pleases, and changes the system of the shop whenever he finds it convenient to himself without considering whether or not it injures the workers. In a union shop the workers are represented by a shop chairman selected from among their own number, and they have a price committee to make prices with the boss. All seemed to be well, but from what I saw in that shop and in many others afterwards, I was convinced that it was not so well as it seemed.

True, the workers have a right to complain against any wrong done to them by the boss, but not all the workers have courage enough to complain against an employer. Most of them just shield themselves behind a few brave workers who carry the brunt of all the criticism. The boss often thinks that the workers as a whole do not care, that only the few brave ones ("trouble-makers" or "kickers," the boss calls them) raise the discontentment of his people, and if he finds it impossible to discharge these few, he makes their lives so miserable that they are forced to leave themselves.

I did not stay long in that shop. The workers had trouble fixing the prices. Work was slack, and the boss said that if the workers would make the garments cheaper he would try to get more work for them. But the people were wise enough not to believe him. When the season is over no more dresses and waists are needed, even if they are cheaper. Besides, if the price on a garment is once made, it is never changed in the busy season. So all the workers refused to accept the unsettled price work.

The foreman, thinking that as a "new hand" I would not have courage to refuse, brought me a bundle of unsettled work. The eyes of all the workers were fixed on me with eagerness. They feared that I would accept the work and break their solidarity. But with a glance I assured them that they need not fear. I took my bundle over to the counter where work was given out and asked for another one.

"What's the matter with this bundle?" asked the foreman.

"It is not settled," I said.

"That's nothing, go ahead. We'll fix up the price all right," he answered.

"I'm sorry," I said again; "I have no right to accept it when others do not."

"So you are also a union member, eh? Now, don't be foolish; don't wait for them; they are kickers; they don't know what they want."

But I would not. "I think they are right," I answered.

"Then I have no other work for you. Do as you please — either take the work I give you or go home."

It was a challenge. The chairman came over and said: "Listen, Mr. Foreman. You'll be so kind as to give some settled work to the girl, or we'll all bring the work back to you."

The foreman answered him with his usual expression, "Mind your own business."

A quarrel began.

I stopped the chairman. I did not want any trouble arising on my account and I said that I had better leave, but the chairman would not let me go; so at last I got a bundle of work. The next day when I came in to work, my machine was out of order. I had left it in perfect condition the evening before and now suddenly it began to break the thread. The foreman was also the machinist and he was too busy that particular day to fix it. My bundle of work was not complete; I was short of some collars. When I went over to the counter and asked for collars, I did not get them.

"The bundle was complete," said the foreman. "You are responsible for losing them."

"But I did not lose them," said I. "I'm sure that I did not get them."

"You did get them as well as every one else got

them in their bundles, and you will have to pay for them if they are missing."

"I assure you that I did not lose them; I only opened my bundle this morning."

"Girls very often take certain parts home and then they come and claim that they were not in the bundle."

"I hope you do not suppose that I took the collars home," I said, feeling a little offended.

"Who knows?"

That was too annoying.

"You may act as you please, but I am no thief! I'm sure that you know best what happened to those collars," I said in anger.

I felt too insulted to speak to that man again and left the shop.

I understood that my machine was out of order through the efforts of Mr. Foreman and that it was also his wish that the collars should be missing. He saw in me a loyal union member and as such I was not desired, so he had annoyed me in order to cause me to leave.

Through the papers I sought jobs everywhere. In some places I was too late; in others my address was taken and they promised to send for me. I tried for other jobs than dressmaking.

I found an attractive advertisement.

> "Flowers and feather-making; good pay, steady position to right party; experience unnecessary. Delancy, corner of Clinton, fourth floor — rear."

I went to that address. An old, shabby building, no signs outside, a very dark hallway. As I climbed up the wooden stairs I had to grope my way, feeling ahead of me with my hands. A sudden fear struck me, as I reached the third floor. It was too quiet for a factory or the smallest shop. A few voices from the fourth floor came faintly to me. I suddenly recalled that nameless advertisements, with great inducements for inexperienced workers, were often traps for girls. Breathlessly, I ran back down the stairs, risking my neck in my mad haste through the darkness. In the street I looked around the building, trying in vain to find some trace of a feather. I never looked for feather-making again.

"Operators on dresses; very good pay; steady work. 145 West 26th Street, 7th floor."

I went there at noon. A few young girls were walking back and forth on the sidewalk, anxiously watching the people who entered the building.

"Are you going up to the eighth floor?" a pretty little blue-eyed blonde asked me.

"No, to the seventh, — why? Anything the matter?"

"We are out on strike for three days and we hope to win if there will be no scabs," she explained, looking at me suspiciously.

The other girls stood behind her. I assured them that they need not fear me, that I would be delighted to help them if I could.

The elevator-man smiled when I told him to stop at the seventh floor.

"You is gonah eight floor, not on seven."

"No, on seventh," I insisted.

When he stopped on the eighth floor, I repeated, "The seventh floor, do you understand me?"

He went down and let me out on the seventh. A man who came out from the office greeted me very pleasantly. When I told what I had come for, he said: "Sure! Say, Bob, take the girl up to the seventh floor."

"Is not this the seventh?" I asked.

"No, the elevator-man was mistaken. Here is the boy — he will take you up."

"Listen, Mr. Bob," I said to the boy when we were on the stairway. "I know we are going up to the eighth floor where there is a strike."

"Yes, they advertise for the seventh so that the strikers may think that the boss has shut up the place, and the people who apply for jobs can go freely up to work so long as it is on the seventh," the boy murmured in my ear, and begged me to keep quiet because he would lose his job if it became known that he told.

I walked on up to the eighth floor.

Three long rows of machines stood empty. At the end of one table, three middle-aged men were bent over their machines. A short, stout gentleman came over to me.

"How do you do, miss! Will you please just sit down for a minute? I will get a machine ready for you. You will find this a very nice place to work in," he said, as he busied himself with a machine.

He did not even ask me what I could do, where I came from, or what for — the usual inquiries to a newcomer. I looked around. I studied the men's faces so as to describe to the workers the men who were scabbing on them.

"Where are your workers?" I inquired.

"Oh, I am only starting this shop. If you have any friends or workers you know of you can bring them in with you. I pay very good wages."

I promised that I would and told him that I would not be ready to start work before the next morning.

"All right; the machine will be ready for you in the morning. Don't forget to bring your friends," he reminded me.

The girls eagerly surrounded me when I came down, smiling, to them.

I gave them all the information I had. A brisk Italian looked up at me approvingly.

"Oh! shu', shu', me know you wuz no scab, you a nice girl. You see, we is striking foh no raise. We no wonna raise; de men upstairs no union men, they no pay dues. They take all de best woik."

She spoke more with gesticulation than with her voice. I could understand neither.

The other girls then told me that the three men upstairs refused to belong to the union. The boss would give them the preference so as to make the union workers envy them, and the men teased the other workers continuously and made fun of their foolishness in belonging to a union when they could get more from the boss for not belonging. When a few days previously, an officer from the union had come up to speak to these men, they had insulted him. As a result, the workers went out on strike, to protest against the men who tried to break the solidarity of the shop.

I sympathized with the girls. I was delighted to hear them speak so enthusiastically.

"Will you permit me to picket with you?" I asked them.

"Of course, sure!" they all shouted.

I forgot that I still had some advertisements to answer. I had never been out on strike myself and here I had a chance to stay with them and help them. True, their strike was not a bloody fight for a better life; it was a peaceful strike, a protest against a few ignorant men who, for a few extra dollars paid by the boss, tried to destroy the spirit of organization and help bring back the old conditions.

Back and forth on the sidewalk we paced, watching the building and exclaiming at the sight of every newcomer, "A strike on the eighth floor; do not go up there; don't go up there."

The policemen would drive us away from time to time. I saw no reason why they did so, as we did not overstep the rules of order.

We chatted all afternoon and I learned every one's story. All of them were immigrants who had come to the land of promised freedom, to the land where people "shovel gold," as Tina, the dark-eyed, charming little Italian had dreamed. She came over here with her father and two brothers to shovel up a lot of money and then return to Italy, where they had left the invalid mother and younger sister. They had dreamt of carrying money back with them to buy a villa and live like real decent people do.

That dream long had vanished. Instead of that, Tina now belongs to the union. She cannot read, but she has learned through her friends that working-people are also decent people, that only the capitalists shovel gold, and that the working-people of all the world must unite to take the unearned gold from those who do not work. She is very enthusiastic about the labor movement, but her great trouble is that she cannot speak English. She told me all this in broken words, gesticulating with her hands and her whole body. "But it's o'right, me go to school nex' wint', me lea'n to speak much, and read all the papers."

Julia, the blue-eyed blonde, came with her parents from Russia. Her father had not had a trade in Russia. Here he had tried all sorts of work, but never succeeded in earning enough to support the family. Her mother would get home-work from some factories, and after the housework was done and everybody was asleep, she would sit with her head bent over the needle trying to earn the small living. Julia had had only one year's schooling. At twelve she took out false working-papers and has been working ever since. Her mother suffers from her eyes lately and cannot sew any more. There is a younger brother whom they keep in high school, so that when he graduates he shall be better off than a "common worker." Julia now is the main support of the family. Her only recreation she finds in the Settlement House on Henry Street, where she has evening classes, music, lectures, and a club.

Lena, also an immigrant from Russia, had had a better life. Her family was independent of her wages and she had the money for herself. She had not cared to finish school, for it was too monotonous, and she went to work as soon as her age permitted. Together with her chums she liked to flirt with boys on the street corner. Her earnings were spent in all the ice-cream parlors along Grand Street and in satin pumps for dancing. How she loved the turkey trot and the tango! The breadth of her world had been confined within dance-halls and ice-cream parlors. The prince of her dreams had been Jake the prize-fighter, whom she had met at a dance-hall. She spoke in a frank but wistful tone, when she told me of her former sweetheart.

"My! how he could dance! His tall, broad figure would sway in time with the music. As he stood beating the time with his foot and his body, one could not help but be proud to dance with him. And he could fight even better than he danced! He had already won his third prize. To be sure, he paid with a broken nose, which spoiled his beauty a little, for he certainly had been beautiful when his nose was straight. But what was that in comparison with his heroism, for he certainly was a hero. All the boys feared him, and my chums — how they envied me! That was four years ago," she added and paused, her eyes wistfully looking into space.

"Then," she continued, "I gave up all that sort of thing very suddenly. Sonia, a girl who sat next to me in the shop, set me thinking one day.

"She was a queer girl, that Sonia. She never took part in our conversations. At lunch-time she would always read while eating. Often while her eyes were eating the book her hand would be reaching out for the food, and she would clutch a spool of cotton or an oil can and bring it right up to her mouth. We had some show watching her at lunch-time. At work she would always hum sorrowful melodies that would make one cry. Everything about her was so sad and thoughtful.

"At lunch-time one day, I showed the girls my first picture taken with my sweetheart. I made Sonia raise her head to look at it. I told her of Jake's heroism that spoiled the shape of his nose.

"She looked at the picture curiously. 'Hm, so your lover is a hero; now tell me what is he fighting for?'

"All the girls burst out in laughter.

"'Why, don't you know?—for a prize, of course, and when he becomes well known he will make good money at it, — take it from me.'

"'For what will he get the money?'

"'Why, for fighting, of course. You get me sick with your foolish questions,' I answered disgustedly.

"'For fighting who and what?' Sonia went on stubbornly.

"I hardly knew how to answer. Who does not know what prize-fighting is?

"'Two strong fellows come together to fight, and when one defeats the other, he gets a prize, either in valuable presents or in money,' I tried to explain.

"'Who pays the prize?'

"'Why, the people who come to witness the fight. This is one of the greatest American sports.'

"'And what are the results?'

"'I told you what, — either one wins or loses.'

"'I mean, what happens to the one who loses?'

"'Oh, nothing; he loses, that's all. Sometimes he loses his teeth, or he breaks an arm or a leg. It is very dangerous to be a prize-fighter. One must be a hero.'

"'To be a prize-fighter one must be a hero,' Sonia repeated, looking fixedly at me, and then asked, 'Are you not afraid to marry a prize-fighter?'

"'Is n't she funny?' the girls exclaimed.

"But Sonia went on. 'Once already he has had his nose slightly deformed, and what if he will one day return home from a victorious fight with his nose smashed altogether, or his legs broken? Will you be proud of him then? Did it ever occur to you that the fellow whom your sweetheart defeats, and perhaps cripples forever, has a mother or a sweetheart or even a wife and children to grieve over him and to curse the man who crippled him?'

"'If you want me to tell you what "hero" and "heroism" mean, I will,' said Sonia.

"But the power started and we began our work. A million thoughts crowded my mind. I could not work. The sport of prize-fighting disappeared instantly, and I thought, What if Sonia is right? What if Jake should break his legs? I was horror-stricken. I saw my Jake no more a hero. I saw him a piteous cripple on a corner in Grand Street begging for his living, and I shook with fear and disgust.

"After work Sonia waited for me to go home with her. Our ways lay apart. She had to take the subway to the Bronx, I had to walk to Grand Street, but she walked down with me and immediately began: —

"'A hero is some one who does something great for the people, who fights for the good and welfare of his country, who fights for people's freedom, like those heroes in Russia who are exiled to Siberia because they fight for a people's freedom; like George Washington who freed the American people; like Abraham Lincoln who freed the colored people from slavery. A hero is one who risks his own life to save some one else — not one who cripples or hurts another for living, or sport. Your sweetheart hopes to make his profession of prize-fighting. Professions and trades ought to be helpful to the human race. A doctor is to heal, not to kill, his patient; a lawyer is to save innocent people and bring them out of difficulties; an engineer is to build better houses, new bridges, more railroads to make it easier for the people to travel. We make waists to clothe the women who cannot sew for themselves. All honest workers make their living by doing something that is good for others. A prize-fighter is like a thief or a murderer, who makes his living by robbing or killing others — and the people who enjoy such sports are like Indians who dance around the fire where they burn white men alive.'

"I swallowed her words with passion; they were high, strange words, some of which I was unable to understand, but Sonia seemed to have hypnotized me. She was so fascinating while she talked, there was such a strange look in her eyes, I wanted her to tell me more and more. She seemed to know such a lot of things.

"From that day on the ice-cream parlors, the dance-halls lost their charm. The world seemed to extend much farther than Grand Street. I no more made fun of Sonia's sadness. I sought her companionship. Everything about her seemed so wonderful, her quietness was so mysterious. We became friends. I learned from her that she and an older sister had escaped from Siberia when they were exiled. They were just three months in this country, working in the Triangle Factory, when that terrible fire broke out, swallowing a hundred and forty-seven young people, her sister among them. She looked wild as she pictured the terror of that fire. Like a mania the picture of her sister throwing herself out of the burning window follows her day and night. I understood now why she was always so quiet and thoughtful.

"She spoke to me about the workers getting organized. I did not understand what she meant, but I enthusiastically accepted it. In fact, I liked everything Sonia liked and I wanted to learn and know as much as she did. I began to read, and soon realized what a worthless thing I had been. I went with Sonia to meetings, became acquainted with a lot more of earnest people. When preparation for a strike began, I threw myself into it, heart and soul. All my energies were now concentrated on organizing workers so as to prevent Triangle fires in the future. There was no end to my happiness when the general strike was won. In my shop alone wages were increased one and a half. — Yes, thanks to Sonia, I have changed entirely. I go to night school in winter and I read a lot in the summer."

Absorbed in her story, which she related in an amusing mixture of her old slang and her newly acquired better words, I had not noticed that it was quite late, the streets were deserted, the workers all gone; even our two little pickets were also gone, while we stood talking.

"And Jake?" I asked, as we turned to walk down the street.

"Yes, Jake, — I spoke to him and told him all that Sonia said and that he would have to choose between me and prize-fighting. Well, he chose to fight. At the time of the strike I saw him among the gang of strike-breakers. I look back now with horror; I realize now that if it were not for Sonia, I might have some day become a member of the underworld by marrying Jake, for only underworld people could accept money for breaking strikes and beating up the strikers who are trying to fight for a human life."

Before we parted Lena said, "You must meet Sonia some day; she will be so pleased to meet a girl of your kind."

"Why?" I asked in surprise. "How do you know my kind?"

"Oh, from the first minute I saw you, I told the girls that you must be somebody! You remind me so much of Sonia, only you are more cheerful, your eyes are so lively, they jump, jump all the time, in all directions, and I like it."

Much pleased with being compared to Sonia whom she adored, I promised that I would be glad to meet her and we parted. But I did not return home. I went deeper down into the slums swarming with Italians, Jews, Slavs, and Mongols. The girl's story deeply impressed me, and puzzling questions rose in my mind. Lena had had an opportunity to finish school. Why did she not? Why did she enjoy flirting on the street corners and prefer the dance-halls and ice-cream parlors?

And as I walked on, nearer and nearer to the tumult, into the hot boiler steaming with trashy humanity, where all sorts of vices can find a splendid hiding-place, as I made my way through the multitude of children that crowded the sidewalks and thoroughfares, through the masses of suspicious, eagle-eyed young men, lurking about and trying to entice the children for their criminal purposes, an answer rang in a loud, poignant voice.

Lena was a child of those streets — to quote her own words: "The streets were always so lively, but school was too monotonous, they make you memorize, memorize — and that's all. Of the forty girls in the class, teacher paid most of her attention to the few brightest ones; with the others she had little patience and was glad to be rid of us when school hours were over. Perhaps, if I had had somebody to make me interested in my studies, I would have continued school."

On questioning her as to her mother's indifference, she answered: "Oh, I was like many other fools who are ashamed of their parents because they don't speak English, or because of their old-fashioned ways. To me, as to many, my mother was only a 'greenhorn,' a foreigner, and, of course, inferior to me, an Americanized girl. — So, you see, my mother had no influence over me."

How many tragedies are there among foreign families where children consider their elders inferior because they fail to acquire the new language and customs! How often have I heard quarrels between mothers and young daughters, or sons, or even tots!

"What do you mean? I am an American — you are only a greenhorn; you don't even understand what I say. What do you know about it!"

And the poor, embarrassed mother would murmur hopelessly, "Eh, Columbus, Columbus!" blaming him for discovering America.

The children are not taught that the traditional customs and old-fashioned ways of their parents may be just as valuable as their modern American ones. In their ignorance everything not American is repellent to them.

"Not being controlled by their elders, being little taken care of in the schools, and living in dirty slums, what becomes of them?" I thought, as I watched the children playing in the streets.

Lena was converted by Sonia. Oh, how many Sonias we need to convert the Lenas!

CHAPTER V

I FOUND a position the following week in a union shop. The cheapest line of waists was produced there, but it was very busy. The girls rushed their machines, hardly having time to breathe. From the shop chairlady I learned that the shop was under good union control and that fair prices were paid to the workers.

Pleased to find a good union shop, I tried hard to increase my speed, but in vain. I was accustomed to work with great care, stopping after each seam to examine it, while here the girls threw out from their machines dozen after dozen of garments without stopping to examine a single article. I liked the shop; also the forelady, a little, elderly, but very lively and energetic, German woman. Her soft German accent sounded so encouraging as she spoke to the girls while passing from one machine to the other, finding some pleasant word for each one of them. Very often the kind creature would get scoldings from the boss. "Miss Smith, you neglect my place too much; the girls behave here as if they were out on a picnic. Can't you, once for all, stop that singing and giggling?"

"Oh, mein lieber Gott!" she would exclaim in defense. "De girls iss young und dey can't help laffing a little."

To the girls she would say: "Please, girls, haff a little sense. Don't laff when de boss is around. Don't you see he gifs me hell?"

Persistently as I tried to quicken my speed, I could not accomplish it. I worked to exhaustion, but did not succeed in making more than $1.10 a day. So I left to look for a better place.

The hot days began, the heat was frightful, and I had severe headaches. There were some shops in which I was offered a position, but for a salary below the scale. I would have accepted a lower wage until the new season began, but I was afraid that by accepting a lower wage the girl who did receive the scale would be laid off, so I refused to accept.

I was soon to part with my cozy little sun tub — my little room on the top floor. The furniture in it consisted of a single bed, a table, a chair, and a small bookcase — my own — with a few books. Some art postals brought from Russia hung on the wall. It was very cozy and clean and sunny, though small, and it was the best I had lived in since I had come to America. The greatest comfort in it was the private door into the hallway. I could come and go whenever I chose, without disturbing the people from whom I rented it, and I had to part with it because I could not spare the six dollars a month for rent.

At that time I learned from some members of

the Coöperative League of a few apartments which are run on a coöperative basis. The rates were very low — $3.50 a month for two in a room, $2.50 a week for board, two meals a day. I found it the cheapest place for me and moved in there, sharing my room with Fannie, whom I had known before.

I liked Fannie for her fearless participation in the "movement." Her activities in the shops where she tried to organize her fellow-workers had often cost her jobs, but she fearlessly went on agitating. She could never bow her head and make peace with the bad conditions prevailing in the factories and she would always protest against the slightest wrong done to her or her co-workers.

It surprised me very much to find her doing housework in the coöperative house. I did not think it more attractive than the shop, nor was it exciting to such a restless person as she was.

I remember, I was asked once why I did not accept domestic work that provides one with a good home, instead of walking around idle for weeks in search of work. In my greatest extremity I would never have considered domestic work. It seemed very degrading to me — the thought of giving up all my liberty for a good home — if it could be called such — where one must serve and obey every member of the family. When everybody is in the dining-room the servant sits alone, eating her dinner by the lonely kitchen stove; when they are all in the sitting-room, she sits alone in the servants' room. When all are out, she must stay in the house; the days and hours for her leisure all prescribed for her. The atmosphere in the shop was slavery enough for me. But if I made my fight by day, I did my work and struggled to gain better conditions for myself and my co-workers. When the shop door closed behind me I belonged to myself. No matter how hard I must fight for my existence, no comfort nor better pay would atone to me for submitting myself to the arbitrary control essential to living as a dependent in somebody else's house. Why I would be nothing but an "I want you."

To my question, why she was doing it, Fannie answered: "Oh, it is not very interesting, but it is less troublesome. I became heartily tired of the continuous struggle against the boss in the shop, always fearing to lose my job because I have the courage to stand up and point out the wrongs done to us. Never sure of to-morrow's bread; slave day in and day out. Eh, my dear, you'll come to know as much when you are here as long as I am."

"But is not domestic service even worse slavery?"

"Oh, yes, it is. I would never go into it except in a coöperative house. I am a member of this house as well as others. They work in the shops — I work here. As little as I earn, I am more contented. I feel free; I am not exploited any more. I fear no boss, no foreman who would discharge me because I sympathize with my fellow-workers. I can go out whenever I please and do as I please with no fear. Then you must consider that I am working here for an ideal to show that coöperation is possible."

It was a hot, suffocating night, one of those summer nights when the air in the tenements is exhausted and all the fire-escapes and roofs of the East Side and part of Harlem are transformed into bedrooms. We lay in our bed unable to fall asleep — inhaling each other's exhaled breath.

"Let's go to the roof," suggested Fannie.

The roof was already crowded. Some were asleep, others sat in groups gayly chatting, amusing themselves with raising and lowering a pitch in accordance with the snoring of their neighbors.

We settled down near a small group who were engaged in a hot discussion about value of coöperative land.

"But here," said one, looking around, "all these people would rather choke with the suffocating city air than go to land."

"Yes, it is true, they would rather stay here than become lonely farmers," was the rejoinder.

"Why are farmers deserting their homesteads for the city? Is it not because their life becomes too monotonous? Why are hundreds of city people who started out on the land returning to the city with their money lost? Is it not because they felt too lonely?"

"There are other reasons for it," said a third. "The city people lack the knowledge and experience necessary to succeed on a farm. And often they have not sufficient money for modern farm equipment."

"We can succeed in bringing back the men to the land only on a coöperative basis. We need to create coöperative colonies, that will furnish congenial society and all necessary equipment, and also instruction for would-be farmers. That is what we need."

I lay stretched on a blanket, paying little attention to their coöperative farms. My eyes were fixed on the view from the roof overlooking the spacious reservoir in Central Park, where the clear blue sky and the bright full moon found their reflections. The gigantic trees threw long shadows over it, coloring the water a dark green. A heavy melancholy swept over me. I looked around me. What was I doing here on this roof among all these people?

I felt the roof, the people, the thick air, as a million-pound weight on me.

My heart, my soul, everything within me was rent in pieces. I devoured the scene with wide-open eyes, as if trying to embrace the high blue sky, the trees, the water, and breathe it, breathe it all in.

My head grew dull and heavy, the sounds of my neighbors' heated discussion came fainter and fainter until they died away — and out of the quietness came soft sweet sounds of a doleful Russian Burlak's song, "Uchnem." Soon I was immersed in the melancholy melody, which caught and carried me higher and higher, close to the sky. I could almost touch it and feel the blueness, were my hands not paralyzed. I was swung in warm soft clouds and lulled by something so charmingly sweet and mournful — until the sounds all died away.

Startled by a deep sigh, I opened my eyes and saw Fannie sitting near me, her hands clasped tightly behind her head, her widely opened eyes looking wistfully toward the east.

The day was just beginning to break, transforming the dark night into the gray morning. A big round spot melted and reddened the horizon. Fascinated, I sat up watching the sun mount.

Another loud sigh heaved from Fannie's heart.

"How wonderful, how glorious nature is!" Fannie murmured wistfully.

I looked down to the reservoir. Its greenish water gleamed out from the trees.

"Let's go to the park," I suggested.

"Yes, let's go down there," she said approvingly.

Quietly we walked down from the roof and off to the park. The streets were deserted, only the clattering of a passing milk-cart or bread-wagon disturbed the silence from time to time.

The leaves and grass were moistened with the morning dew; the fragrance all around was deliciously sweet. The birds singing and twittering their morning songs greeted us merrily.

Assured that no policeman was around so early, — for it is forbidden to lie on the grass, — we spread our blanket near the reservoir and leisurely stretched ourselves on it.

"Oh, Lisa, how wonderful it is to be able to enjoy all this!" she said longingly. "I hope that you won't spend your youth in the shops."

"You don't want me to graduate into domestic service!" I said indignantly (that traditional, disdainful feeling about domestic service strongly clinging to me).

"I do not mean that, you little idiot. I am speaking of your appearance. You can graduate into something better and more worth while," she added, looking at me with envious admiration.

I looked up at her. Nature had really been a little severe with her — a very romantic soul, she longed for love, for admiration, but was often unnoticed. Having no desire to discuss myself, I turned our conversation to something else.

"What about your activities, Fannie? Did you give them up with the shop?"

"Oh, no, not at all. I only grew tired with the

slowness of the trade-union movement. Those peaceful agreements only tie the workers up. The trade-union motives are too conservative. Their only demands are for shorter hours and for a raise in wages."

"But, Fannie, that means so much," I argued. "The shorter hours in the shop enable us to devote more time to our spiritual development, the raise in wages enables us to get more wholesome food and worthy recreation. With time and money the best things can be accomplished."

"But it goes so awfully slow!"

I could not dispute with her very much for I considered my knowledge of the trade-union movement not complete enough to defend it.

The sun had risen high when we started home. I did not like to leave the park, but in my ears still rang the words of my one-time foreman — "If you think that you can live on nice mornings or May holidays, do not come in to work."

No, I could not live on beautiful mornings. I had to work in order to live, — I knew that, — and again I started out to look for work, knowing that my work would pay me only for a bare subsistence, not for a living.

CHAPTER VI

IT was hard to find a job on dresses or waists at that time, but I recalled that the season on sweaters had just started. I got a morning paper and found a job through the advertisements. It was on Grand Street, on the ground floor, in a room at the back, with two small windows facing a dark, narrow yard. Two knitting-machines occupied almost the whole length of the room. On the side there stood a table with five machines — two pocket and facing, one cutting, one button-hole, and one button machine. The space between the table and the wall was only wide enough for the chairs to be placed. I was given the last machine. After working three days, I asked the price. The boss told me to wait until Saturday so that he could test my worth.

The conditions in that shop — it looked more like a stable — were terrible. It was swept only on Saturdays, for in order to sweep it some articles had to be moved and that was too much trouble for the middle of the week. The dust and lint from the wool were inhaled instead of air. I could hardly speak in the evening, my throat would be so clogged with wool.

Here again I met with the same type of girls that

I had met in my first sweater shop—I once more came in contact with the queens of imitation. There were only four of them, very young girls, but their high pompadours and their paint and powder added years to their faces. In those merciless hot days, when the perspiration pouring down would leave grimy streaks alternating with blotches of powder, their faces were grotesque. Their paleness, their thinness, all about them bore the imprints of their sweated labor conditions, but they cared little. In the evening, as soon as the power stopped, powder-puffs were extracted from stockings, faces were smeared again, the aprons changed for the latest style of short hobble-skirts, and off they went to pace Grand Street, the East Side Avenue.

I waited until Saturday and again asked for my price. My boss, who had evidently been in the business but a short time, asked me to wait another week.

"I am sorry, but I can't stay for a two weeks' test," I said. He offered me six dollars a week. "What! Six dollars for such a hard week's work, fifty-four hours of life in that dirty slum?" I cried in angry surprise, enraged by his offer. "Give me my pay, please, I shall not stay here a minute longer." He did not give me the pay, and after an hour's bargaining, I remained for nine dollars a week. If I had only had a few dollars to tide me over the dull season, I would never have remained there for any amount of money, but I saw six weeks of idleness staring me in the face and that determined me. I hated the place, I hated the boss. I pitied the girls,—driven and scolded by that miser of a boss, they accepted everything without protest. Their self-respect was lost under the weight of ignorance and bad conditions.

"Why don't you wash your hands?" I asked them, seeing their unwashed, oily hands touch their food.

"Oh, you expect us to wash our hands when we have only half an hour's time?"

"Why not? It is more important than to powder your faces during the half-hour," I answered. "Your cheap powder and paint ruin your faces and your unwashed hands poison you."

"As if you won't use any powder," they said, looking suspiciously at me.

"I surely do not," I said; and I went on, giving them my bit of knowledge of hygiene.

Their suspicion changed into confidence and they began to like me.

In our daily conversations I tried to discover if they had any knowledge of workers' unions.

They knew there was a knitting-workers' union, but they had never cared to know more about it.

"Why don't you join such a union? Is it not worth while to fight for a shorter-hour day? Is it not important to have an hour for lunch so that you could wash your hands and rest a little before you resume work? Do you know what it means to your health to work in this room?"

"Hey, hey, there! Stop talking! Time is money!" would come the voice of the boss from the other corner.

"Sure it is!"—I found satisfaction in mimicking his tone. But talking had to stop. How I wished that the season on dresses would begin so I could leave that hateful place.

I began to attend the regular meetings of the Waist and Dressmakers' Union so as to follow up the news of the trade, but not much could be learned at them. The time was taken mostly by a few discontented members who interrupted the meetings to accuse the union leaders of dishonesty. They were prejudiced by their bosses through the sort of lectures I was often given on the unreliability of the labor leaders. Their minds were poisoned and ignorant of the facts. If a complaint was taken up and the case was decided in favor of the manufacturer, they would ascribe the decision to treachery on the part of the leaders, and nothing would convince them that they were wrong. Many of the members protested against those few for killing their time, but it was impossible to quiet them. Each succeeding meeting was less and less attended.

I did not know the leaders at that time. I

thought that they might possibly lack ambition or energy to push matters for the members; they might be to blame for not understanding the people thoroughly; but I was sure of their honesty.

As I could gain so little from the meetings, I thought I would study the trade-union movement from its history, but with fifty-four hours a week in that disagreeable sweater shop, I was too tired to do any other work. My evenings I spent in my favorite corner near the reservoir in Central Park. Sundays, friends took me out bathing.

Another girl who came to the shop to do the same work as I, inquired of me about the work and the salary to be expected. I told her all I knew and of my experiences with the boss.

"You be careful; he will surely try to bargain with you for two weeks," I said; adding: "Is it not a pity to sell fifty-four hours of your life in such a place for nine dollars a week?"

"What do you mean?" she asked, not understanding me.

But from the other side came an angry voice. "Hey, hey, there! Stop talking! Time is money!" and I had not the chance to explain to her any further.

On Saturday, when the girl asked her price, she also was offered six dollars.

"Why, am I slower than the other girl?" she inquired.

"Who says you are?"

"Because she gets nine."

"Who says she gets nine? Hey, hey, there! Come over here! Who said you were getting nine dollars a week?"

"Why, of course, I am getting nine dollars a week; you yourself are paying me the money."

"It's a lie," he said; "I never pay that much for this kind of work."

My eyes filled with rage at his words.

"You should be ashamed to act that way!" I cried out. "If you would pay me a thousand dollars, I would not stay in your shop a minute longer!"

So my term ended and I still had to wait a few weeks for the season on dresses.

Oh! how I hated to enter another sweater shop, but I had to. After about two weeks in two other shops, the heat, the dust, and the filthy surroundings drove me from them, and I decided to stay home until the season on dresses started. I felt guilty walking around in the park those mornings. It seemed as if I had no right to enjoy the fresh air, the trees, and the flowers, for I had to get work. But I could not enter the sweater shops again.

I was so happy when one of my friends found a position for me on samples. Now, I thought, I shall be settled at last.

In that little shop there were only four of us

including the forelady. She was a very thin, pale-faced woman of about thirty. She appeared to be tired out from her long years of work. Her big round blue eyes looked very dull, her face bore traces of past beauty. I sympathized with her and wished to be friends with her, but she did not treat me very friendly. She seemed to be envious of my youth, for I made a big contrast to her — I was full of life, each vein, each move of mine beat with life. I do not know what feeling she had toward the boss, but she seemed to feel hurt if he happened to smile at me. The forelady would try to put me back in my work. Realizing that she did it purposely, I thought it better to leave. I was not worried now the season had started and it would be easy to find a job.

With bitterness in my heart I recall that summer of so many unwilling adventures which I had encountered in my endeavor to get settled at work. When I left the last shop, I found a job as draper the next day. It was an independent union shop. About sixty people worked there. All were pieceworkers, even the finishers, and I was told that all earned good wages. There were four drapers, who earned from twenty-six to thirty dollars a week. I only made a dollar and a half the first day, and in the evening the boss called me over and said: —

"Listen, little girl. I like your work very much, but you are too slow. I need the quickest hands."

"Oh, but this is the first day. I will work much more quickly when I am accustomed to it," I appealed to him.

"I am sorry, but I am in a rush with my work. Can you run a machine?"

"Oh, yes, I am a sample-maker."

"Then I have a job for you. The jobbers for whom I am doing contracting need sample-makers. If you wish, you can go up there in the morning to work."

The next morning I reported to the place as directed. All the work was made by outside contractors, who sent the finished garments to the jobber's office, where they were packed and shipped to the customers.

The designer liked my work and paid me the sample-worker's scale — fourteen dollars a week. Fourteen dollars a week! Was I not fortunate? I thought. I sat calculating and planning how to manage it. I'll manage to live on six dollars, hire a teacher so I can study English, spend a dollar a week on opera when the season opens, and save the rest.

I was happy, very happy.

My new boss, the jobber, was a very sickly man, so that his wife was the actual manager of the place. She was very harsh. All day she would just wander from the office into the sample-room, from there to the packing-room, from the packing-room to the show-room, and back. Her unpleasant, commenting voice would be heard continuously. Even the boss feared her, and would shrivel in her presence. With young girls, however, he behaved much more bravely and, seizing favorable moments when his wife was not around, he would flirt with the models and the packers and often act very shamelessly.

Nor did I escape his attention. One morning when I was alone in the sample-room he came in.

"Good-morning, my dear."

"Good-morning," I said quietly, busying myself in my work so as to cut off any conversation, for I did not like to be alone in the room with him.

"My! what curly hair you have! Is it not beautiful!" he said, beginning to smooth my hair. I blushed and moved away. "Do not be afraid, I will not hurt you," he whispered, his eyes wandering all over me. "What a wonderful form you have. If you were only a few inches taller, you would make a perfect model, would n't you?" His face melted into an impudent smile.

Again I moved away in indignation, but before I could open my mouth to speak, his wife stood in the open door, her eyes filled with rage at her husband. He shrivelled and immediately slipped out of the room.

"So you are flirting with an old man — for shame!"

Tears came to my eyes, a lump swelled in my throat.

"Why, I — I did not know that he would dare behave so to me," I cried out, gasping for breath.

She laughed. "You act as innocent as a nun, eh, sample-maker? Now, you get your hat and go. This is no place for you, you sample flirter."

"I have given you no right to abuse me that way," I said, through my tears.

But she would not listen to me.

"Go on! Go on! Your pay will be ready."

I put my hat on. "Oh, you are a madwoman," I said, and rushed out.

Tears were flowing all my way home, and when I reached my room I broke into hysterical sobs.

"What happened?" Fannie asked, trying to comfort me.

"Oh, Fannie, does it pay? Why, why must I suffer so much? Am I an idler? Don't I want to work? But why, in order to get work, must we endure insults and humiliations?"

"Now, now, calm yourself! What is the matter?"

I told her all that had happened.

"Just think of what I have gone through this summer! A new job almost every other day, small wages, sweat-shop surroundings! Oh, Fannie, it is outrageous! Where will it end?"

A deep sympathetic sigh answered my despair.

"Why don't you get married, Lisa? You are so

young, so full of life. It's a sin to waste it. You are so pretty you would make an ideal, darling wife."

"Is that an ideal? Is marriage the remedy for the working-girl? Why, it is ridiculous, Fannie! You are too intelligent to talk like that. The kind of man I shall marry is likely to be a poor wage-earner, also exploited as we all are, and our lives would be miserable under the present conditions. As for marrying for money — you know what I think of marriage without love. Above all, I believe in the economic independence of women. Conditions must be created so that the girl shall not be driven from the shop. The long hours, the unsanitary conditions, the small wages, the frequent slack seasons, drive the self-supporting, unprotected girl sometimes to a life of shame, sometimes to suicide, and more often to marry any one who proposes to her. She finds that the easiest way, and she goes on breeding human stock for misery's pleasure. Eh! What an ugly, contemptible world this is! I am trying so hard to bring my family over here to save them from the Russian autocratic teeth, but I would rather see my sisters dead than see them enduring humiliations from such a debauchee as that jobber. Brr! It throws me into a fever when I think of it."

When my nerves quieted a little, I went out and aimlessly wandered around until I found myself on Riverside Drive. On a bench facing the Hudson, I sat for a long time, absorbed in thinking. Am I not to find a decent place where I can work and get a living wage? Is my appearance to prevent me from keeping a job? I hated my face that day, because it had attracted that clumsy fool and had made me lose my job at fourteen precious dollars a week.

The thought that I had to go out early in the morning and look for another position, the fear that I might get a shop similar to the previous one, made me so unhappy that I felt I could much easier jump into the Hudson. Yet work I had to get. During the last six weeks I had had only two scanty meals a day, for I had to provide car-fare and could not spare a dime for lunch. My younger brother was soon to arrive from Russia, and I would have to help him.

The sun had already hidden her last golden rays; twilight fell upon the Hudson. I still sat on the bench, having no inclination to move. The warm, pleasant evening rapidly enfolded me, spreading its mysterious beauty all around me. I sat as if in paradise — in comparison with my room where the air was so choking this hot July month.

Boats — all kinds of them — swam up and down the river, leaving the water wavering in long strips behind them. Their noise allured me — it made me homesick. It reminded me of past days when on the river at home, bordered by willow trees, we would row and sing in the quiet evenings. Sometimes our young, happy voices were caught by the wind and carried away to the older folks, who sat quietly after a day's work, resting on benches near their homes. Far out on the river away from civilization, away from the gendarmes, we gave vent to our revolutionary songs — songs of our future freedom. Filled with hope, our voices went ringing higher and higher, echoed by the wood near by. How sweetly those days had passed, days full of hope, full of wonderful faith in the future! And here I sat now, broken-hearted, disappointed, tired out. "Life! Life! Oh, happiness where is thy sweetness!" A mortal anguish swept over me, wrapping me in a heavy melancholy, dragging me down to the waters where the many little fires of the "Palisades" took their evening dips in the dark, quiet waves of the Hudson. That spacious river below, those beautiful stars above, the graceful trees around me — oh, the glory of it! I drank it, drank it to intoxication.

In my ecstasy I would not have thought of leaving the park had not my stomach called for food. I had had nothing to eat since early morning, so I made my way toward home.

CHAPTER VII

I WALKED along Riverside Drive past the colossal hotels and beautiful private homes. No light was seen in any of them. It was a pity that such comfortable homes were empty most of the year. Their dwellers fly from one country to another, from one resort to another, to spend their time. They never worry for bread, they never fear to lose their jobs, they never wander in the parks with hungry stomachs. They have people — thousands of people — in mines or factories or stores, who sweat for them, who hammer out the gold, or dig the coal for them, and they easily spend the wealth, never giving a thought to the hard labor of so many thousands of people, who, with their happiness and often with their lives, pay for the pleasure of those few who spend their lives in long vacations and eternal luxury. "How many people of the East Side, how many families cooped up in tenements, could enjoy these vacant comfortable dwellings and this lovely air of Riverside Drive and Hudson River!" thought I. "Here the houses stand of no use to anybody. Oh, how unfair, how unfair, the present system of life is! Here am I — willing to work, to earn a decent living, willing to sell my hands, but get nothing, while those who never work have more than they need." Did I envy the rich that evening? Oh, no! I hated them! I hated them! for they were worse than highway robbers — robbers who fear nobody in the world, who rule the world with their iron power. And the world tolerates them!

In the morning I found another job as draper, but only for a few days. It was a protocol shop. The drapers worked on an optional system — some were week-workers, some were piece-workers. If a piece-worker refused a price offered by the boss on a certain garment, that style was made up by the week-workers — the system created competition between the two classes.

When I asked the chairlady who represented the workers why she allowed that, she answered, "Oh, I can't help it; the girls don't care themselves, and I can't waste time in making them see that they injure themselves."

"But can't you speak to the boss?"

"The boss purposely wants to keep one worker against another. When I spoke to him, he told me that he runs the business as it best suits him. If the girls would care, I would complain to the union."

If the times had been better for me, I would have stayed there and tried to help do away with that system, but I needed money badly before my brother should come, and working there I could not make very much at the start, so I left.

The next job I got was on Spring Street. It was a very small place. I had to make samples and do the draping and a good many other things. After two days the boss came to me and told me he needed some one to watch the few girls, but as his place was small he could not afford to get a forelady, so he wanted me to take charge of the operators. The finishers, he said, he would look after himself.

I refused without hesitation. How could I become a *forelady?* That would mean to carry out all the instructions of the boss, for I could not keep such a job if I did not obey his orders. I would have to hurry the girls with their work, I would have to bargain with them on prices and always take the bosses' side, offering the girls less than they deserved. I would have to order them to work overtime when they were tired from a hard day's work.

"Oh, no, not I, I could not do it," I said to the employer.

"Then I'll have to look for somebody else who will do it," he said.

I got another job that same day. It was on Madison Avenue. I remember the place was so light and clean. The foreman, a middle-aged, kindly-faced man, treated the people fairly. For the few days I stayed there, I never heard him shout at a girl. My salary was to be thirteen dollars to start with. On Saturday, after work, I went to the foreman, asking him if I could possibly get my pay, for I was in need and could not wait until Tuesday — the regular pay-day. The foreman told me it was against the rule of the house to pay money before Tuesday, but he would make an exception with me. In a few minutes he took me into the office and told me to wait until my pay was made out. As I waited, the boss came in — a tall, handsome young man with a wealth of dark bushy hair and big round blue eyes.

"What is it you are waiting for, young lady?" he asked.

I excused myself for asking for my pay on Saturday, and explained to him why I needed the money.

When the bookkeeper had my pay made out she left. I still waited for the money. The boss sat at his desk writing. I had no courage to disturb him, so I sat and waited. At last he stood up, straightened himself, and smiled at me.

"So you are in hardship — too bad, too bad." Then he took my pay, looked at it, fixed his eyes on me, and asked: "Is that all you get?"

"No, I get thirteen, but this is only for two days and a half," I said, already regretting to have aroused his pity.

"But, my dear girl, that would not be enough for you. Don't you need more than that?"

A thrill ran through my body when I noticed

how he was measuring me with his eyes while he spoke. I felt what that glance in his eyes meant. It was quiet in the shop, everybody had left, even the foreman. There in the office I sat on a chair, the boss stood near me with my pay in his hand, speaking to me in a velvety, soft voice. Alas! nobody around. I sat trembling with fear.

He spoke. I did not hear what he said. Instinctively, I stood up and stretched out my hand for my pay. "Wait a moment; I will give you some more." But no more had I time to refuse when he grasped me in his arms.

I screamed, and with superhuman strength threw him from me and ran into the hall. Luckily, the elevator stopped at the same moment as I rushed out of the office. I ran into it.

Breathless and pale, I reached home and madly ran up the stairs. The people in the house were alarmed seeing my paleness, but I gave no explanation. In my room I closed my door, hid my face in the pillow, and cried, cried all afternoon. How I hated men, all of them without exception! I stood up before the mirror and studied my face, trying to find out if there was anything in it that awakened men's impudent feelings toward me. I hated my youth, it had caused me so many painful humiliations. When I went into the dining-room, I thought all the men there followed me with the same rude looks as that vicious boss. If I could only discredit that man so that he would never dare to insult a working-girl again! If only I could complain of him in court! But I had no witnesses to testify the truth; with my broken English I could give very little explanation. Besides that, if I were working in a shop and were called to court, the firm might suspect some evil in me and send me away. So I left him alone and never went to collect my money, although I was in a frightful need.

Before bedtime I cried again.

"What is the matter now?" Fannie asked.

She knew nothing. I was ashamed to tell her the truth.

"I lost my pay on the way home," said I.

"Oh, you stupid thing! You should be more careful with your money."

"Yes, I was careful, very careful; that is why I lost it."

I was so sorry for those few dollars which could do me so much good those dark days.

I could not sleep. The day's events vividly appeared before me, and in the silence of the night my shattered nerves started their nightmare trick — shrinking, wrangling, jumping, heaving, splitting my head. Hideous long shadows gathered about, dancing wildly, screaming with laughter through their gnashing teeth. Hands — hundreds of hands with sharpened nails — stretched out to me. They danced, they laughed, they screamed, they conquered.

Sunday, going out to Bath Beach with a friend, I was introduced to an aunt of his. When she learned I was out of work, she gave me a card to her brother, who was a jobber on waists, and whose son kept a small waist-shop in the same place. She assured me that through her recommendation I should get a job.

On Monday morning I was up early. The thought of a new job made me so uneasy that I could hardly sleep. My bitter experience with my last shop pictured me all the bosses as vulgar and rude as the one from whom I ran away on Saturday. A religious mood possessed me that morning. In my despairing helplessness I blindly sought for a higher power whom I might invoke for protection. If there was an Almighty he should at last turn to us, the insulted ones, the humiliated, the searchers for everyday bread. But there was no such God, or else he would not tolerate such misery! So many shops I had tried in a period of eleven weeks, and what did I find? Shops where people were treated as slaves — shops where workers looked like shadows, with symptoms of tuberculosis — shops where young girls were subject to the vulgar and rude desires of some scoundrel bosses. Oh, how dreadful, how dreadful!

But I had to forget it all. My brother was already on his way to New York. I had to provide some money for him, and there I stood penniless. I had to find a job and try to keep it if I did not want to starve together with him. For myself I cared not much, but my younger brother — for him I was responsible.

"After all, I'm not the only one," I thought. "I'm one of them! One of so many thousands of young girls, who struggle so hard for their everyday bread, whose youth and beauty fade in those hateful shops without a ray of happiness."

I made up my mind to devote myself to the work, not to care for the surroundings, not to think of the rights or wrongs.

I went with the card that the woman at Bath Beach had given me to her brother, and got the job.

The first few days I was so absorbed in my work that I did not even notice the people with whom I worked. I spoke to no one except the girl who sat next to me, when I needed to ask anything about the work. I noticed she was a good worker. She told me that she had been employed by this firm for the last three years, and was a sort of forelady over the few girls who were not competent in the work. She also had made all the samples before I came. All she was getting was ten dollars a week. "And I hope to get a dollar raise," she said with pride. She also told me that she had been a dressmaker in Russia.

"Goodness!" I thought, — "she — a dressmaker from Russia — three years' experience in the same place — making all the samples, a bit of a forelady, and gets ten dollars a week! What could I, not being a dressmaker from Russia, not having three years of experience, nor titled as forelady, expect to get here?"

Though I knew that my work was good, — the foreman liked it, — still I feared that he might not pay me more than nine or ten dollars. But I sat still; I did not ask for a price until the week was over.

Although absorbed in the work, I nevertheless raised my head from time to time to observe the surroundings. The place was on the first floor. Its length extended from Seventeenth to Eighteenth Street. In the Seventeenth Street front was the shipping department; the Eighteenth Street end was taken up by the office and show-room. The very dark middle space gave shelter to the small factory, its windows facing narrow courtyards. Sunshine could never reach them, the buildings being so high and close to each other. We had to work by gas-lights from morning till evening. The windows and the sink were covered with dirt an inch high; they were seldom cleaned. The table with the machines stood close to the wall, and we had plenty of dust to inhale from the windows and the yard; also the smell of the rotten sausages of the "Busy Bee" restaurant which was in the next basement.

In the middle of the week two girls left. They were the best operators. Sadie, the girl next to me, told me that they only stayed there for the dull season. Now, when it became busy, they went back to their old places.

"For, you see, in a union shop they make more money in the busy season," she said.

(So this was no union shop! My chance!)

"Does it pay for you to stay here?" I asked. "Don't you think you could get a job for fifteen dollars a week, such an experienced worker as you are?"

"Oh, I know I could," she replied, "but I am not going to leave this place. The boss has promised to make me his forelady." (To become a forelady was her highest ambition.) "He also wanted me to get him green girls for help. You know he does not like the Americanized girls — they fuss too much, and very often make trouble in the shop, while green girls are quiet and don't kick about the pay."

"And do you get green help for your boss?"

"Surely," she answered. "Almost all the girls, except the few Italians, I brought here, as soon as they came over from Russia. Don't you think the boss is a fine man? He told me he likes to give a chance to the poor green girls, who don't know where to look for work."

"And how much does he pay them?"

"Well, the first three weeks they work for nothing. Then he begins to pay three dollars a week, raising a dollar or half a dollar every season. Now, excuse me, I have talked too much. I've got to work," she said, bending down her head to the machine.

She began to rush in order to make up for the loss of the few minutes' talk she had with me.

My mind was full of thoughts. I forgot that I determined to think only of the work. I could not keep the promise to my own self. I looked at the girls around the table, and I thought of them! They were all so youthful, — most of them were seventeen, eighteen years old, — as yet not hurt by hard work, and what did they get? Three, four, or five dollars a week; perhaps some of them a little more than that. And how they were rushed, and scolded by the foreman, who sometimes used such language that would make a Russian Cossack blush! And how did they live? Did they also, like me, walk around in the street sometimes a whole day, without a single meal in their mouth? Did they also, in the hottest summer days, passing by a restaurant, stop to inhale the smell of delicious roasts which awakened such a painful hunger in the stomach? With pain in my heart I felt that their youth will with no mercy be crushed prematurely under such conditions, and I had a desire to talk and warn them.

When the week was over, I asked the foreman for a price. He nearly fainted when I told him I wanted fourteen dollars a week. It was fortunate for me that the two girls had left in the middle of the week, for the foreman, being very busy and having few skilled workers, was afraid to lose me, too. So after two hours' bargaining, I remained there for thirteen dollars a week, but was strongly forbidden to tell anybody in the shop of the "extravagant amount" I was getting. I was the highest-paid worker in that shop.

CHAPTER VIII

NOW that I was getting such an "enormous amount of money," I could afford to buy lunches. But I was saving for my brother, and could only spare a few cents each day. A peddler used to come every noontime and sell food to the girls. In his small basket he had bread, sardines, sausages, and salmon. I bought a box of sardines for six cents and some bread. The very same day I was seized with terrible cramps which put me to bed. I suppose my stomach was a little weakened from the weeks of irregularity in my meals, and could not digest the cheap old sardines. The doctor took my case very seriously. He told me to follow the prescribed diet: fresh chicken soup, fresh eggs, and cooked fruit, nothing else; then be out in the fresh air in the morning as long as I could.

I smiled. How naïve those doctors were! Where could I get fresh chicken soup every day? Surely not in the coöperative house, where we paid two and a half dollars a week for board! And fresh air? Oh, I had had enough of it during the long dull season.

In three days I grew so pale, so thin, that when my friend Clara saw me, I frightened her.

"What happened?" she asked in anxiety.

I told her of my stomach trouble.

"Why did you not come up here and stay a few days with mother until you felt better? How could you go to work, feeling so miserable?"

I explained to her it was impossible for me to stop for a day even, because my brother was coming the end of the week and I needed the money; then I feared to lose my position, for it was a very busy time, and some other help would be taken in my place. That evening she did not let me go home.

"You shall not stay uptown any more!" she said. "Now you'll get a room where it will be near the shop, and the car-fare you'll spare for better food."

At the end of the week my brother came. Poor brother, he was so disappointed when he saw my pale, thin face. He expected to find me strong, healthy, and happy. Happy I tried to be.

"Is it the work that affected you so badly, sister?" he asked the first evening.

"Oh, no," I answered; "it is only a cold that I got. It'll be over in a few days."

He sighed, bowing his head, and continued: "You know that mother is still crying, when she thinks how hard you have to work, and she always fears that you have nobody to look after you. She still thinks that you are not able to do your own washing, nor mending, nor ironing."

"Don't worry," said I. "At home when I had

mother and sister to take care of me, I knew nothing, — but now, I have learned everything, and get along fine!" ("Get along fine!" . . . Well, I had to lie for his sake.)

For the next few days I was very busy searching a place for my brother. I finally got him a position in Brownsville with a plumber. As it would be too far for him to travel from New York, I also found him a room and board near his shop. Myself, I moved downtown, not far from the shop. Though I bought better food, I still felt very weak. It seemed that the two dull seasons during the past year and a half had undermined my health. I had never felt sick until this recent breakdown.

The worries about work and my brother had occupied so much of my thoughts for the past few weeks that I had even forgotten the existence and importance of the union. When I became stronger, I again started to attend various meetings and lectures.

The shop was a model of a "sweat-shop" in the full sense of the word, — narrow and dark and dirty. When it happened to rain, our clothes felt damp all day long. The owner cared very little for the shop. He was always busy with his jobbing. (A jobber is one who gets ready-made merchandise to sell.)

Only two or three experienced operators were kept; the rest were mostly green girls, and were always called "learners." Even those who stayed there for more than a year were still called learners. We worked in sets. Each skilled operator had two or three learners to work with. The latter would work, each one on a certain part of the garment, and the skilled operator would complete it.

Those poor learners were never given a chance to learn to make a complete garment, because the work went much quicker when each girl worked on one part continuously. Also, because a skilled girl would not stay for the small salaries they paid. But a learner, lacking skill, would be afraid to look for other jobs, and she was thus dependent on the man for whom she worked, being obliged to accept any salary paid to her.

The foreman was unusually respectful to me because I was the highest-paid worker in the shop. But the greatest respect he began to pay me when he happened to learn through the papers that I was to play on the stage. (I still belonged to the Dramatic Club at that time and we gave performances every once in a while.)

"So, so, you are to become an actress — it's fine, very fine," he would say proudly.

He informed the girls that I was an actress, and they also began to pay me more respect. That helped me in gaining their confidence. I often tried to convince them how much better it would be for them if they would all get together and join the union. They were glad to do it, but they were afraid of the boss. To sit quietly and see the way the people were treated was impossible. I had two girls, helpers, under my direction. I was forbidden to bother much with them, but I could not help instructing them in the work. My teacher's temperament was aroused unconsciously. I would give them every day a new part of the garment to make up so that they could learn how to make a complete waist. When the foreman noticed it, he scolded me for the first time.

"I don't pay you for teaching the girls how to work. I don't want you to bother away your time. I want to have my work done!" he cried in anger.

"But how can I work with them when they don't know how?" I would argue.

He would not listen. My heart pained me for the girls. One of them was paid three and a half, the other five, dollars a week. Both together did not get as much as I. When I worked alone I could only make seven or eight waists a day; together with them, I used to complete a bundle of sixteen, sometimes eighteen, waists a day. I told the girls how much I was getting. They did not believe me. They could not think of such big pay.

"Why should not you tell the boss that we are worth more?" they would beg me.

I did speak to the foreman about it. I explained to him how much work was given out and how much they deserved according to the salary I was getting. He opened his eyes wide at me.

"Why, who allowed you to tell the girls how much you are getting? And what is your business to worry about the others? They ought to be glad we took them in here. Where else could they get a position when they don't know how to join a seam?"

He was enraged. I understood it was useless to argue, and went back to the machine.

There was another girl in our shop, an experienced operator, who came for the sake of her sister, just recently arrived from Russia. That girl, Mollie, got twelve dollars a week and her green sister, five. After two weeks Mollie's sister, becoming accustomed to the system, began to give out as much work as Mollie herself, but she still got the same pay, for she was called a learner, and a learner was only raised each season. Mollie spoke to the foreman about her sister getting a raise, but she was only laughed at. Both of us decided to report to the union office and ask their help. I had succeeded in getting six girls who were ready to join the union and we hoped to get the rest later on.

On a Friday evening, just a week before Labor Day, we went down to the union office. There by the complaint window of the independent department I gave full information about our shop and asked, if possible, to have a committee sent to take us down on strike so that we could get the people to join the union and then put our demands before the boss. The man by the window promised to attend to it. Every day the next week I waited for a committee, but it did not come. On Wednesday evening I went to the union again. The man by the window told me they were too busy, that we must be patient and wait.

The next morning, when I sat by my machine, two strange men, together with the owner, entered the shop. They looked all around, tried the lights, and made some remarks about the windows and the sink. I surely thought they were people from the union, and told the girls so. But they were not, for in a few minutes we were told to stand up and march out when a whistle should blow. Later I learned that they were sent from the Board of Sanitary Control to give us fire drills.

I was puzzled. How did the Board of Sanitary Control come to send a committee to a non-union shop? I knew that the board was created by the union and the Manufacturers' Association, and had nothing to do with the non-union shops. There must be a reason for it.

In the evening I had a talk with the girls. None of them knew anything about it. They did not even know from where and for what those men came. They were all interested, — even Sadie, the future forelady, stopped to listen to us. I made all kinds of suppositions.

"Perhaps," said I, "the union sent up those men to find out how the shop looks before they take us down on strike."

"What do you mean by strike?" asked Sadie in surprise. (She knew nothing of our plans.)

I was afraid to tell her anything, for she would surely report to the foreman, and I would be fired. At that time I had worked only six full weeks and could not afford to be fired. I still had to help my brother, who did not get more than five dollars a week. On our way home Mollie and I decided to wait till after Labor Day. Then if the union had not sent anybody, we would go up there again.

Sunday morning when we came to work (we observed Saturdays), the foreman had news for us. The boss was going to change the week-work system for piece-work right after Labor Day. All the girls, with the exception of a few, were shocked with the news. As the foreman would always tell them that they did not deserve the money they were getting, they feared that on piece-work they would make still less.

After work I tried to comfort the girls. I told them that now was the best time to make a union shop. That we would get a price committee to settle prices, and they would make twice as much as they had made before.

On my way home I thought of the change the boss was going to make. A sudden thought seized me.

I recalled I had read in Saturday's paper that the Manufacturers' Association sent out letters to all its members who practiced the week-work system, and informed them that by the request of the union they would have to change their system to piece-work.

"My boss must belong to the bosses' association, then," I said to myself, "or he would not have changed his system so suddenly." And how could he have those men from the Board of Sanitary Control unless he was a member of the association? The more I thought of it, the more I concluded that it must be so.

Tuesday evening Mollie and I went over to the union, and I found that my boss really was a member of the association.

So when I went in the next morning to work, I walked over to the foreman and told him all I knew about the boss, the change of system, and the shop, and that now, if he wanted us to do piece-work he must send for a man from the union to settle prices for us; otherwise we would not work. The foreman stood looking at me in embarrassment. To him everything came unexpectedly. He knew nothing of our preparations, and my explanation took him unawares.

"Who told you to go to the union, you foolish kid? The boss has nothing to do with the union — with all those fakers! It is true that the boss belongs to the association, but what do you need the union for? The poor girls don't have enough to eat, — how could they afford to pay dues and fill the union leaders' pockets?"

I was tired of that song. I had heard it so many times from different bosses and foremen.

"Please," I said, "don't you blame the leaders. I never saw them and they have nothing to do with our demands. We ourselves want to have a union shop. Your boss cares to belong to a bosses' association; we care to belong to a workers' organization! Besides, if you are so sorry for the girls why don't you pay them according to their worth? You drive them like slaves, and what are you giving them in return? Three dollars a week, in addition to scoldings! You make them believe that they are not worth even that much!"

I was enraged, and gave vent to all my feelings. If the foreman had not interrupted me, God knows how much longer I would have spoken.

"Look here!" he said, "I thought you were a nice, respectable girl. I did not think you could be so fresh. We don't want you to make trouble in this shop. If you don't like it, you can go. You are only a new hand here. Those girls are working here more than a year, some more than two years, and they never spoke to me like that. I was to them like a father — and they'll admit it, too. I did not think you'd have the nerve to agitate the people against me and the boss!"

All the girls were sitting by their machines shivering with fear. They were afraid the boss would fire them wholesale. For the first time I saw them cowards as they were. When the foreman turned to them, asking if they had anything to say, they all bowed their heads, no.

"See!" he said to me; "nobody cares for a union but you. Take my advice and go to the machine and mind your own business! We'll fix up the price without a man from the union."

All that time the boss stood at the door of his office and listened to everything. It seemed that he made up his mind to leave all to the foreman, for he said not a word, but an hour later he came out and, passing between the tables, addressed the foreman.

"What was the noise you made this morning? You know that I don't like trouble in my shop. If there is any girl in here who is displeased, let her go. Nobody keeps her here. I want no market in here."

(He spoke as if he did not know who that girl was, though he saw me speaking to the foreman.)

The foreman pointed me out to him.

"There she is. She wants to call the people out on strike. She is the one who keeps them back from work."

I stood up.

"I don't keep them back from work!" I cried

out; "but we have a right to know what we are working for. When we were week-workers, we knew how much we were getting; now we are piece-workers, and we want to know how much we can earn. It is no more than right we should know." Then I added, "Don't you know that in each protocol shop there should be a chairman and a price committee selected from the workers to settle prices with the boss?"

He grew mad.

"Who are you to make rules in here, you little kid? You are only a child. What do you know about it? Do you think you are in Russia fighting the Cossacks? Go to Russia and fight the Cossacks! I will not allow you to make me revolutions in the shop and spoil the people!"

I went to my machine, not saying a word. Every minute I expected to be discharged.

CHAPTER IX

THAT day was the most miserable one I ever spent in the shop. The foreman quibbled at everything, scolded me, and cursed the union leaders — as if it were their fault! I could not work. I felt so insulted, tears were running from my eyes, the work slipped out of my hands. In any other circumstances I would have left that shop, even if I had to starve, but not at present.

"Should I give in?" I thought. "After all, the boss was right; if the girls don't care, why should I? But they do care; they are only afraid; they have no courage to start; their courage is killed by the miserable life they live. Why should I not try to awaken their dignity, their self-consciousness?"

In that choking atmosphere, working by gas which inflamed the eyes so badly, with not a single ray of sunshine all day, there we sat working for others. Oh, how I wished to stand up and cry out to the world of all the misery we are submitted to in the shops; to show them the causes that so often drive girls to hell-life; to tell them that the money the bosses acquire through our labor is criminal money! It comes from the starvation of the people; it is the happiness, the youth, the beauty, the blood of many, many innocent, unprotected working-people!

Impatiently I awaited the lunch-hour, when I ran over to the union office. With tears in my eyes I told them what had happened. The complaint clerk made out a complaint to the association against my boss. He advised me to call the girls to a meeting. With meeting cards in my hand, without any lunch, I returned to the shop. On the cutting-table sat the foreman, all the girls around him, and he amused them with his tales.

"Come on here," he called. "You may also listen to it. . . . When I was in the contracting business for the cloak manufacturers, I had to deal with the union. Once, when a business agent came around to find out if everything was in order, I invited him out for lunch with me. There in a saloon I treated him with a few beers so that after lunch he was not able to walk out. When he stepped out of the door, he fell like a dead one on the sidewalk. Then I called over my workers to show them who their leader was. I also told them that for one beer he would sell the union. That's what your union is," he concluded.

But I stopped him; I could not stand it any more.

"A thing like that never happened, and if it did, you played a very mean trick on that poor man!" I cried out. "Girls, don't listen to him — he wants to poison your minds, that is his only aim!"

I tried to control myself. I respected his age — he was old enough to be my father.

It is hard to describe how I spent the rest of that day. He called me "damn liar." He wanted to make the girls believe that I was an agent from the union, that I was paid by the union leaders to get money from the girls for union books.

I could not control myself any longer. Tears burst out of my eyes. I took my hat and coat and wanted to run, — run away from there, from all the trouble, I was so excited, — but Mollie held me back.

"We don't believe him; we know his aims all right," she said. "Don't go; if you go, this place will remain as it was. Now you have started it, bring it to an end. The girls will stay with you."

I did not go. I sat by the machine, but could not work. My mind was too upset. At four o'clock I distributed the meeting cards, calling everybody to the meeting. I warned them if they did not go, they would regret it. Half an hour before the power stopped, the foreman called Mollie and me over to his table. He was all changed. His manners, his voice, were so soft, so polite, that it made us wonder. In a begging tone he began: —

"I want you girls to understand me. The boss does not care to keep up his shop. If he is to pay higher wages to the girls, he will not be able to keep a foreman and he will give up the business altogether. He can make a nice living without these few machines. I will be the one to suffer! I'm only a poor man, have to support my family. What am I to do if he does give up the business?"

My grudge against him disappeared instantly.

Poor man! I pitied him. After all, he was only a tool in the hands of the boss. He also worked very hard. The boss's son would walk around all day long from one table to the other, of no use to anybody. He did not even know where to get a spool of thread when a girl happened to ask him for it. And he was the one to get the profits. The foreman, who had managed the shop and who had done the cutting also, only got as much as could be taken off from the girls' worth.

But I could not help him. Were he a fair man, not a coward, he would not make his living out of the girls' money, for, as he himself said, the boss kept him as long as the girls got small wages. I said to him: —

"If the boss will give up the business just because he has to pay decent wages, let him do it! For three dollars a week the girls can find a job anywhere!"

After work I waited for the girls to take them to the meeting. Sadie, the forelady, fearing to spoil her future career by attending the meeting, refused to go. Another girl followed her. The three Italian finishers were also afraid to go, so that we only had nine girls at the meeting.

I succeeded in explaining to them the situation as it was. I assured them that if the boss should give up the business, it would not be for the reason that we want too much, but for the simple reason that his son is not able to manage the business, and if it is so, let him do it. Such brilliant jobs as they had they could always get.

They elected me as shop delegate; also on the price committee, together with Mollie.

The next morning when we came in to work, the boss was already there. He changed his policy. Without addressing anybody, he began to talk.

"Oh, I have nothing against the girls' selecting a chairlady. Let them also select a price committee, but they could do all that without a union. They need not belong to the union and spend their money."

I went over to him and introduced myself as the shop chairlady. I told him that we had appointed a price committee and were ready to settle prices, but with a man of the union, because we had never settled prices before and we wanted to have an expert.

The boss realized that further arguments were useless and he finally agreed.

Until a man from the union could come up, we continued with the work. I still had my two helpers. Now that I was no week-worker, I had liberty to instruct the girls in the work. After a day or two they worked alone and did well.

On Sunday I asked the foreman to give me some work that I could work on without interruption. I wanted to time myself, to make a sort of test, and see if I could possibly settle the prices myself without any help from the union. I wanted to do justice to both sides. The girls should be able to go on with the work, without any loss of time, and the boss should have his work done in time.

On Monday, when I had the work finished, I went over to the foreman to speak about the price. Somehow we agreed on the price of the style I tried out. All were satisfied. The day passed very happily.

In the evening the foreman told me to remain to settle some more work. I did so, but instead of prices, he spoke to me of something else.

"Listen, miss! I know you are a sensible girl, and you deserve to get more than the others. You need not bother with the union. I myself will give you a chance to work yourself up. See, as you are on piece-work now, you can keep your two girl helpers as before. You'll pay them as much as I paid them till now. . . . Think what you can make on them; the work will all go through you, and they'll work through your hand! You need not be afraid that they'll refuse. If they do, I'll get other girls — there are always plenty of them!"

Should any one throw stones at me, I would not feel as hurt as I felt while he spoke. It was the worst kind of an insult I could ever feel. He wanted me to become a sub-contractor, to give me a chance to advance myself! In what a way! By cheating the girls! In the same way as I had been and still was cheated!

At last the deputy clerks from the association and the union came. I was called to the office. In my broken English I tried to explain to them. After me the foreman spoke. Hearing him talk in the office in a soft, gentle voice, it could hardly be believed that he could use such violent language as he used in the shop to the girls. He denied all I said. He told them that as long as he had been foreman in the shop, the girls had never complained of anything — that peace had prevailed until I came; that I also was satisfied until the system of week-work was changed; since then I had begun to make trouble in the shop because I did not want to work piece-work.

"It's a lie!" I interrupted him, maddened by such false statements. "I'm glad that the system is changed — I only wanted to have a man from the union to settle the prices for us!"

He lied through and through, and I could not help saying it was a lie, but in saying that, I only succeeded in discrediting myself, for the clerk of the association stopped me.

"Why, that girl is unbearable; she has an awful temper!" he said to the clerk of the union. "After all, he is the boss of the place, and she should have more respect for him! She is too fresh!"

"Oh, if you only knew him!" I said, and burst into tears, for it hurt me that he was trusted more than I.

Both clerks failed to see the impossibility of selecting a girl in our shop. All the girls, without any exception, were as week-workers very much underpaid. If any girl was to make a test, and be paid by the hour according to her former salary, we would surely not be able to gain anything, but I was not given any chance to explain it to them, for they were in a hurry and left.

When I stepped back into the shop, the girls were waiting impatiently for news, but before I said a word, the foreman anticipated me.

"Well, girls, even the clerk said that she was fresh, that she had a bad temper. He also said that I'm the boss here, and she has nothing to say!"

So he interpreted the clerk's sentences, and wanted the girls to believe him.

In the evening on our way home, I had all the girls around me. Some had the greatest sympathy for me, but Sadie and her friend saw their enemy in me.

"What do you want the trouble for?" she asked me. She did not have sense enough to see things as they were.

CHAPTER X

THE next morning the first thing I did was to remind the foreman that we were to select a test girl. I hated him so much that morning that I would sooner have talked to the Devil. Can any one imagine being friendly to a man who tramples on your dignity, who tries to drive you from the shop? But I tried to be friendly in order to get a test girl to make the prices so the girls could get their pay.

There were only four girls who were competent enough in the work to act as testers. From the four he selected Sadie and wanted nobody else. How could I agree to her when she was such a good worker, yet got only twenty cents an hour? My arguments did not do any good. He again called me "trouble-maker" and "fresh girl," and when I went to him for work, kept me waiting purposely to make me lose time.

At lunch-time I went to the union again. There I cried for a long time until I was able to talk. The people up there comforted me. To them it was not new. Hundreds of girls used to come to them with the same grievances as I. But those did not cry any more. They were accustomed to being ill-treated for their union activity. Time and experience made them take things easier; while I was only a novice.

The assistant chief clerk immediately made out a complaint against my boss for ill-treatment of the chairlady and promised to have the clerks sent up right after lunch; but I was not willing to go without the clerks. I knew what awaited me. The assistant persuaded me to go alone. He also told me that in case the deputy clerks should not succeed in settling the trouble, the case would go over to the chief clerk, and he would either make an end to the trouble or close the shop.

I went back to work. Before I had time to sit down, the foreman began again.

"Well, what did your union tell you? You think I'm afraid of you, eh? The more you complain, the worse for you! I shall give you such work that you will not be able to make two dollars a week!"

Sometimes there were styles of which parts had to be sent to the hemstitchers outside. (My boss did not keep any hemstitching machines.) If we got a bundle of that work, we could only make it ready for hemstitching. To keep the girls busy, the foreman would give to each girl two bundles — one with hemstitching, the other to be completed, so that when a girl had her work ready for hemstitching, she would work on the other bundle until the first work was returned.

That day the boss gave me only such bundles as

required hemstitching. I would work only for half an hour and then was obliged to sit idle until its return. When I asked for a bundle that I could work on without interruption, he refused me. I complained to the boss. The boss came over and asked the foreman why he did not give me work, but the foreman had thrown the few bundles he had into the girls' baskets and said to the boss that I would have to wait until he would cut some more work. I showed the boss the extra bundles the girls had in their baskets while they had plenty to do without them. The boss took a bundle from a girl's basket and put me to work on it. To the foreman I heard him saying: —

"You better stop troubling the girl too much!"

When he walked away the foreman said: —

"You see, girls, now, what good friend she is to you! She is so mean she grabs your work from the baskets while she herself has a full basket of work!"

That exasperated me — I could not stand it any longer; indeed, I had a full basket of work, but I could not make it up for the main parts of it were out to be hemstitched.

"You are a mean blackmailer!" I cried out. "You only seek to discredit me before the girls!"

To the girl from whose basket the work had been taken for me, I said that I would gladly give the bundle back to her if she thought I had taken her work away. She did not take it.

At three o'clock the clerks came again. When the complaint was read before the boss, he said he knew nothing about it. He told the foreman to treat everybody alike. The foreman again denied everything, claiming that, on the contrary, I had insulted him. He brought in my basket to show them how much work I had and accused me of still kicking despite plenty of work. But when I explained that nothing could be done with the work until the rest of it came back from the hemstitchers, the clerk of the union took a stand against the foreman. He, being experienced in cases like mine, understood the game of the foreman. To him it was not new; he himself had had similar fights with bosses and foremen when he worked in the shop. But the clerk of the association, who had never worked in a shop, had no idea of how people were treated, how they suffered, and he could not believe all my "tales" — as he called my statements. He could not sympathize with me, for he could not imagine that such things could be done! Still, they were; I did not even tell a third of what we endured from the foreman, because time was limited and I wanted to have important disputes straightened out.

In the presence of the clerks we selected a test girl. She was Mollie, of the price committee. They told us that in case we would not agree on the test, they'd have a man sent up to make the prices.

When they left, the boss came over to us and said: —

"Look here, girls, you wanted the clerks and you had them! But I'm telling you again that you may have a thousand clerks to make prices for you, I will not pay a cent more than I pay you now! I cannot afford to pay you more, for I sell my merchandise cheap and I can't raise the price on it."

"Then, why don't you tell that to the clerks? What's the use of bothering around and wasting people's time for nothing?" I asked. "You sell your merchandise cheap, you compete with other firms, and you want us to stand for it? No, we will not! We ourselves gain nothing from it and we spoil the prices for the girls in the other shops; for each manufacturer in order to meet competition will treat his help in the same way as you do, and the other girls, who, for so many years struggled and fought for better conditions, will have to suffer on account of us! No — a thousand times, no! If you are a member of the association, you can afford to pay as much as the other members do; if you can't — all right — give up your business! Somebody else will have to make up the work and we'll get our jobs all right!"

"A — ah, is that what you want?" cried the boss in anger. "You want to drive me out of business — you socialist, you anarchist, that's what you are! Go, go! Your place is in Russia, to fight the Cossacks!"

(I don't know why he always sent me to fight the Cossacks.)

"I'm telling you girls again," he continued, "if I have to pay more, I'll give up the business! If you suffer afterward, it will not be my fault, but hers!" He pointed his finger at me.

"You, Mollie, go ahead, make the test, and let's see how it'll come out."

Mollie was given two waists to test. At the same time the foreman gave two waists to Sadie. He did not trust Mollie, though he said that she was a good, respectable girl.

Mollie tried her best to make the test a fair one. Sadie, who saw her chance to show her devotion to the boss, rushed the work terribly, and when she saw that she was not ahead of Mollie, she had the girl next to her help her out. I watched them all. Sadie had her waists finished ten minutes before Mollie. Of course Mollie's test was not accepted. According to her test, the waists had to be priced at forty-six cents apiece; according to Sadie's, the waist came out at thirty-five cents. All the boss wanted to pay was thirty cents a waist.

When the expert came, he priced the waist at fifty cents. He said that for a waist like that, fifty cents was paid in all union shops. The boss refused to pay either price. He claimed it was impossible for him to exist. He made a proposition to have the work made in sections. The garment should as before be divided into collars, cuffs, bodies, sleeves, belts. Each part should be settled by the dozen, and each part of the waist should be made by a different girl.

I did not agree to it, neither did the union clerk. I tried to make the girls see the danger for them in section work. No skill is required. Anybody could learn in a week or less to make a certain part of the garment. The girls, not being skilled workers, would always have to depend on that one shop, and, of course, would never be able to take a stand against any wrong, for fear of losing their positions.

Again he condemned me for holding back the girls. He would file a complaint against me to his association. As witnesses he had Sadie and his other week-worker, who testified that I had threatened the girls to make them join the union and that I had stopped them from work against their will. The other girls were afraid to say anything. I began to grow disgusted with them. For two weeks we had worked and I had made only nine dollars.

The association and the union at last took more interest in the case. For three days clerks would come and go, come and go; they could not come to an understanding. At last the boss announced that he would give up the business.

Some of the girls began to blame me. They said that they would rather work there than have nothing. I tried to assure them that they would find better places, but the foreman would agitate them against me. Again he would tell them that I purposely raised trouble in the shop to harm them. He announced that those who were willing to work for the price the boss would pay, should stay; those who were not, might go.

Again I had a meeting with the girls. All the will-power I possessed I used to the utmost that evening in convincing the girls of the great mistake they would make if they consented to work under old conditions.

In the morning when we had our work finished, we told the foreman that we would only work there if we had a strictly union shop with union conditions. He announced that no more work would be cut and that we were free to look for positions. I took all the girls with me and went to the union office.

I felt responsibility for them, and there was nothing in the world I would not do for them so they should not regret their old shop. The assistant chief clerk told us that the case was already in the hands of the chief clerk, and I would have to wait for a definite answer. He also advised that none of us should look for another job until we heard the final decision.

We sat in the union office the whole day, but could not get a chance to see the chief. He was too busy with many similar cases. I was told to come in the next day. My girls began to grow impatient and displeased.

I begged them all to stay home next day and not worry. And all that night I lay awake thinking how to get positions for them in case the boss really closed his shop.

CHAPTER XI

AT nine o'clock the next morning, I was in the union office again. The assistant chief clerk told me that as the manufacturer had not informed the association of his intention to give up the business our manager considered it a lockout, and had filed a complaint against the firm. At ten o'clock the deputy clerks went with the complaint to the firm, taking me with them. The boss informed them that he was discontinuing manufacturing because he could not pay according to the decision of the deputy clerks. So the case was dropped.

Going back to the union office, I sat there again all day, waiting for the chief clerk to tell me what to do. Many, many girls with similar grievances were sitting in the office, waiting for the union to help them. The disgust and sorrow in their eyes was so deep! All of them were so young and so pale. "Why is life so hard to them?" I asked myself. "Is it their fate to fall victims of life? Why? Why? The spring of their youth they spend in shops creating luxuries for others, the later years they spend in dark, choking tenement-houses, starving with their husbands and children three quarters of each year. At forty, they are already old, weak and unattractive. Their days are so gray, so monotonous — and so their lives are lived. Under the heavy burden of poverty, their dignity, their self-consciousness, their ambitions are killed. Why don't they rebel? Why don't they stand up against those who enslave them — against those who kill their human spirit?"

"What is the matter, young lady?"

I raised my head. Two very kind eyes from a sympathetic face looked at me. I was so absorbed in my thoughts that I had not noticed a man standing near me. He was the manager of the "Independent Department" and also one of the first leaders to organize the Waist and Dressmakers' Union. For the first time I spoke with a union leader face to face, with a man who was the father of our present organization.

"What are you worried about?" he asked. "I'm watching you for quite a few minutes; your face is so troubled."

His voice was soft, his face so extraordinarily kind, with so much sympathy for me. I told him all my troubles. He sighed.

"Oh, yes," he said, shaking his head, "for so many years I'm in this movement, for so many years I spend my days and nights trying to help the enslaved ones, and still the same old story, the same hungry faces, the same dim eyes follow me, day in, day out. If the workers would realize their position how much better it would be for them. — I'm looking at you now and I am thinking of the many sweet young faces, the many enthusiastic souls like yours, I saw only recently. Those very faces, to-day, are so changed, their youth is faded before its time. My heart bleeds looking at them. — And you, you are also to be brought to the altar of capitalism, and you are so young, so charming. Fight, my little girl, fight against all who would injure you. Let them pay too high a price for every bit of happiness you lose."

For two hours we talked. I almost forgot for what I had come to the union. His friendly conversation filled my heart with warmth.

At five o'clock the chief clerk came from the association. He told us the reason he could not give us a definite answer was that he did not believe our boss was giving up manufacturing. Once previously he had done the same thing; he kept a shop on Division Street, where horrible conditions prevailed, and when his employees began to organize, he claimed that he was giving up business. When the workers had all left the shop, he then opened a new place on West Eighteenth Street. Suspecting that he would play the same trick again, the chief clerk insisted that our boss should resign from the association, so he should not have its protection any more and the union might know how to treat him. The shop was given up and we really had to look for other jobs. I wanted to speak to the chief clerk to ask his advice what to do, for I had to give an answer to the rest of the people. And I feared that they would not understand the situation as I did. But there were so many committees waiting for him that he could not spare me a minute more. He asked if I could wait until the committees were all gone. I gladly sat waiting, because I was very anxious to have a talk with him. I was also very much interested to hear what the committees from the various shops had to say.

For the first time I heard the shop chairladies, who represented the workers in their respective shops, put their complaints before the chief clerk. Many of them spoke with much bitterness, many spoke with disgust of the protocol. Under the machinery of the protocol, their complaints would often linger for months and months before they could be decided. While in a non-protocol union shop, complaints were always decided in the first or second week.

I watched them all. I also watched the manager, being anxious to find out how he dealt with the various difficulties, how he advised the people, and how much he, himself, was really interested in everything.

With tightly closed lips, knitted brows over his eyes that were deeply set in their orbits, the expression of his face seemed severe. There on a chair he sat, listening to the committees. His appearance was in great contrast to the other manager. I watched him rather suspiciously, for he was one of the men of whom I had heard tales of his riches and the valuable diamonds he had obtained since he had become a labor leader. He appeared a simple, strong-built man, with a fighting spirit and much will-power. His voice was loud and clear. To me he seemed a little unfriendly, for the other manager spoke so softly and intimately and seemed much pleasanter.

I waited for a long time until the last committee was gone. It was quiet in the office, and most of the officers had left.

"Oh, what a hard day's work I have had!" he said, taking a deep breath. — "Well, little sister, can I be of any help to you?" asked he so softly I was astonished. The harshness of his face disappeared so suddenly, it seemed to have left with the committees. From under his knitted brows two gray eyes filled with enthusiastic fire looked at me. His lips widened into a pleasant, almost childish, smile.

Before me now sat a man whose hair had turned gray, but his face was so youthful, — a kind, sincere face, — it was hard for me to believe that he was the same man whom I had seen only a few minutes ago, sitting on the same chair, with such a severe face. I asked him the reason for the change.

"My friend," he answered, "having such a hard

day's work, such a hard fight on two cases as I had: fighting with people who know they are wrong, yet will not give in, with people who are trying to get the best of the agreement, and who, themselves, violate every provision of it. It's maddening. Coming back from the association tired and exhausted, I find so many committees awaiting my help, their sufferings, their helplessness impress me so that had I the strength of Samson, I would destroy the present damn world." The last words he pronounced grinding his teeth. "And that is what made me look so angry, severe — as you say. Would the workers only realize their strength and know how to use it, we could revolutionize the world in no time. We need to create a new, a better world."

For a long time we talked. After he had promised to help me to find jobs for the girls, our conversation took a more personal character. I was anxious to know his opinions on many things and I also wanted to know a little about himself. My many questions he answered with delight. He was a man who had grown up in the labor movement; had spent a life full of activity in the trade-unions, a man whose sole object was the advancement of his class. A child of the working-class, a worker himself, he struggled together with them, shared their sufferings as one of them. He also told me about the different unions and their lost or successful strikes, of which I knew so little. He spoke much about our Waist and Dressmakers' Union, expressing his views with optimism.

Mr. Baroff entered the room. "Are you still here? It is so late."

"I captured her attention and we have been talking all the time," answered Mr. Polakoff.

I rose from my chair. It really was late. I had not noticed how time had passed, being so interested in our conversation.

"Be here to-morrow, and we'll find jobs for you and your girls." Both of them promised to do it. "And if you are really interested to know what the protocol is, you begin to study it attentively, and if there is anything that you do not understand, I shall gladly explain it to you," said Mr. Polakoff, before we parted.

I felt happy that night. A new world seemed to open before me. The meeting with the managers enlightened my mind and filled my heart with enthusiasm for the labor movement. In my ears rang, "Fight, my little girl, fight against the world, against those who insult, against those who injure you." These were the words of one.

"Did I possess the strength of Samson, I would destroy this present damn world," rang the words of the other.

So, for the first time, I met two people who were the heads of our organization, two union leaders — one the symbol of love and kindness, the other the embodiment of strength and determination, and just as much kindness that was hidden deep in his heart.

And these labor leaders — were called "fakers." According to the statement of the bosses, who saw in them their bitterest enemies, those labor leaders lived on the "people's backs." The bosses tried to impress this on the workers' mind in order to sow distrust in the movement, and in many cases they succeeded. Ignorant people would take the prejudiced statements for granted and would either refuse to join the union, or those who belonged would accuse the leaders of dishonesty and would disturb the members' meetings in attacking them without reason, without facts. A great many of our members forgot that the union leaders are selected from among the ranks; they are not given the leadership because of their aristocratic family connections. They are given leadership because, through long years of self-denial and suffering for the labor cause, through tireless activity in the "movement," through enthusiastic fights for the rights of the workers, they have proved their energy and their ability to lead. The members often forget that the leaders of to-day are only the co-workers of yesterday. Instead of assisting, of coöperating with them, they fight them. People who would give their lives for the "movement" were called traitors.

The next morning when I came to the union office to meet my girls, who waited impatiently for results, the manager of the "Independent Department" had called up a few shops inquiring for positions for the girls. The first two positions he got I sent up two girls, one a competent worker and the other a learner. Before I sent them away, I took a promise from the competent girl to take care of the other. A few I sent to answer advertisements in the paper, and they found jobs for themselves. Mollie and her sister I sent to the shop where I had first learned the trade. Through my recommendation they got employment there, where one of the sisters is still working.

At home that day I was surprised to find my brother in my room.

"What has happened? Are you not working?" I asked.

He told me that he had a scrap with the boss and left. It shocked me a little, for I knew how hard it would be for him to find a job, as he was strange and did not know the language. Just at that time unemployment began (October, 1913). Hundreds were walking around idle. After Christmas the unemployed were counted by the thousands.

"What are we to do, in case he does not find work?" I thought. For the last five weeks having trouble in my shop, I had earned so little that the few dollars I had saved during the previous weeks were all gone. I would not have enough even to pay my rent, if I did not go to work immediately.

I scolded my brother for his hastiness. I tried to make him understand that a learner must be more obedient. He was not a real learner, he had had some experience at home, but as a matter of fact every newcomer is considered a learner.

The reason why he left his boss was, as he said: "Is it not enough that I work for almost no wages at all? He should, at least, respect me a little more." (He did not know that those who get the least money, get the least respect.) "He is using me as an errand boy, as if I were only fourteen years of age. Besides, his language to his helpers is so overbearing, really, I can't stand it."

I argued with him for a long time trying to make him understand that we must bow our heads and wait patiently until we were able to stand up against the abuses. I also told him what I had gone through. He was shocked.

"Why, you? You were scolded and abused? You, who were loved and honored in the family, respected by every one in our home town, you took quietly the insults of those old clodhoppers?"

"I did not take them quietly; they were imposed on me," I replied.

Tears stood in his eyes. "I could never imagine that," he said in a trembling voice.

He promised me to be more careful in the future, but back to the old shop he would not go.

To reduce my expenses, — for I did not know

how long my brother and I might be out of work, — we moved together into a small room on the fifth floor, somewhere on Ninth Street. Meals I made myself for both of us.

Fortunately, we both found positions the next week. An acquaintance of mine, working on samples in a large firm, took me up there. It was a non-union shop. As I learned later, the union had had several fights with that firm. The firm refused to recognize the union, and in order to punish the strikers, the boss opened factories in the country around New York, sending all the work out there, thus compelling the people to return to the shop on the old terms.

The firm had practiced the same method several times, whenever the workers made an attempt to organize themselves. When, in 1909, the first general strike of the Waist and Dressmakers' Union was called, the firm closed up the shop altogether, getting their merchandise made in the country shops. Later, when the strike was over, the city shop was reopened, mostly with green Italians who worked on the old conditions. The union had made several attempts to organize the country people, but had always failed. The workers were American girls, most of whom were partially supported by their people and did not feel the pressure as self-supporting girls do. They worked for any pay given to them. In other words, the parents worked for their children while the children worked for the employers; neither parents nor children reaping a just reward for their work.

In 1913 when the general strike was called again, the firm succeeded in holding back the sample-makers, who were twelve in number, by reducing the hours and raising their wages a dollar more than the union demanded. Securing the sample hands, who supplied all the country shops with samples, the firm continued manufacturing without interruption, getting the work made outside of New York.

I was the thirteenth sample-maker. We worked in a large, light, airy room, our salaries were favorable, and we were never fined for coming in late. But if it was pleasant in the sample-room, it was terrible in the factory; the prices were so small that the most expert could not make more than ten or eleven dollars a week, while the average operator made no more than seven dollars a week. With the exception of a few Jewish girls, they were all Italians and, as usual, closely related to each other.

When the organizer in our union learned that I worked there, he wanted me to try, if possible, to get the girls to join the union. He still hoped to organize the place. It was the end of October, just when the slack season was beginning, so I risked losing my position. Still, I promised to try.

CHAPTER XII

NOW that I was provided with work again, I had time to think a little of myself. For a long time I had not had any recreation. Before, I had not had any money, and then I was too busy to think of it. The coming season in the dramatic and musical world promised to be very interesting, and I longed so much for a good opera or play. If food was necessary for my physical hunger, music and drama were necessary for my mental hunger.

At that time the Century Opera Company gave operas at popular prices. When I had paid my debt to my friend Clara, I at once went to the opera house and spent five dollars for tickets at twenty-five cents each, so that if I happened to lose my position and be out of money again, I should, at least, be provided with tickets for the next few weeks. I also secured tickets for the Manhattan Opera Company, where Pavlova was dancing at that time. But the highest price I paid for Caruso. He would often cost me a few lunches and dinners that I went without in order to save enough to buy standing-room. I would go right from work, to stand in line for general admission. If it happened to rain, my clothes would be soaked through and through. With wet clothes, I would stand through the performance, changing from foot to foot, while there were always some empty seats in the orchestra. Very often, I would pay with a cold the next day. But the magic of the music was so great, that I forgot the cold as soon as it was past and went again at the next opportunity.

The opera house was the only place where I envied the rich. I did not envy them their expensive clothes, nor their diamonds. I envied them their comfortable chairs which often were empty through most of the performance. People would frequently come in during the second act, and leave at the beginning of the last. Some of them would yawn all through the performance.

Of course, the greater part of the audience sat listening to the opera with much pleasure. But many sat as if it were a duty to listen to the music. They impressed me as coming only to show their latest, and indeed very becoming, fashions.

Besides the theatre, I also attended different lectures on modern literature, of which I am so fond. My favorite authors were Ibsen, Maeterlinck, Prshebishevsky, Andreev, Strindberg, Gorky, and many others.

At home, in Russia, I always had time enough to read. In the small town where I lived, there was no library. (There was a small, unimportant library in the public school, but only for the pupils, not for the public.) In the cities were good libraries, but they were closed the most part of the year, and Russia thought it unnecessary to install libraries in small towns. Our town was big enough to keep two monopol — stores of vodka — that drink bringing ruin upon the people, but not for a library to enlighten the people's minds.

A group of us, young boys and girls, got together and from our own money, after a long time of hard effort, created a small library, hoping to increase it from time to time. Not being able to get a permit, we had to keep it secretly. But the chief of police soon learned of it. He immediately paid us a visit, searching for revolutionary literature. The result of his visit was the destruction of our library, at that time worth two hundred roubles, and the arrest of many of our members. The worst of all was that he sold our books to his gendarmes for ten or fifteen cents apiece, and we could never get them back. We were left without any literature at all — and that was such a painful blow, but only one of the many I had received in my native land — Russia.

How hateful the word Russia [1] sounded. The ignorance in which Russia was trying to keep her people, the many obstacles she put in the way of my nation, — particularly the limitation of civil

[1] Not as a country, but as an autocratic Government, I hated it. The country itself is very dear to me.

rights for us, — the desecration of our lives and private property, that the Government practiced upon us so often, the severe persecutions, kindled fires of hatred in our hearts that burn for a lifetime.

When our library was destroyed, we began to think of some other way of getting literature, for we could not be without it.

Many of us began to subscribe to weekly magazines which gave us very good classics as premiums in addition to the magazine. Some subscribed for a monthly magazine, "The Modern World," in which many of the modern writers appeared. A few of us had friends in the city who supplied us with books through the mail. We would usually read and discuss together, — that helped us in widening our ideas and understanding what we read. If any one happened to visit the city, he or she would attend lectures, also the theatre, and would come home with a fresh supply of impressions, with the criticism of the lectures and performances, and share it with the rest of us. Difficult as it was for us to get what we wanted, still we succeeded in reading the best classics, Russian and foreign, also a great deal of the modern literature. Our teachers, who came from the city, would be astonished at our wide knowledge of literature. As a matter of fact, we, who met with such difficulties in getting knowledge, knew much more than most of the city students who had the privileges of the best libraries.

Since I had left home, I had done very little reading. The struggle for existence, the worry about work, the trouble in the shops, had occupied my mind and time. But now that I was a little better off financially, I gave myself up entirely to reading. I often visited the Public Library; I was not accustomed to being served so readily and receiving every book for which I asked. And if I hated New York with its palaces and slums, if I hated it for its many capitalists, I gave it full credit for its Public Library and Museum of Art.

It was there that I found my coveted *America;* it was there I found *freedom* and *equality!*

With what a sense of adoration I would behold that colossal building of a wonderful architecture! That sacred temple which holds safe within its walls the inexhaustible treasures of knowledge, light.

A worshipping mood often possessed me as I crossed its threshold. In happy bewilderment I would stand gazing amidst the glaring candelabra, high pillars, gliding balustrades, and the picture galleries. The Goddess of Light seemed to flutter in the enchanting silence.

And on the shelves around — on the shelves, safely tucked up for immortality, where lie the brain-children of the world's geniuses, — 't was our inheritance! 'T was for us their wisdom, for us their celestial illusions, their secrets of love and joy, of sorrow and hatred. We — all of us — are the heirs, and if my eye was sometimes disturbed when looking up the front entrance at the carved names, Astor, Lenox, I said to myself, "Never mind Astor, never mind Lenox — 't is ours, ours — everybody's!"

After three weeks of prosperity my brother again lost his job, and I had to help him for the next four months. Had I not lost my position, we could have got along somehow; but after five weeks I was discharged. I once before mentioned that my boss had two shops in New York. The conditions in both, with the exception of the sample-rooms, were terrible. The prices were cut lower and lower, from day to day, and finally thirty of the more brave people in the other shop could not stand it any longer and they went on strike. As soon as they were out, I received a letter from Mr. Baroff, the manager of the Independent Department of our union, who wanted me to try to get my people to join in the strike, for if we did not, the workers in the other shop would lose their strike because their work could be made in our shop.

I promised to do all in my power.

I spoke to the girls in the sample-room. I explained to them that if the sample-makers would stop from work the designers would have no samples for the country shops. And if the boss could be made to realize that he cannot make all his work in the country shops, he would at last recognize his workers as an organized body.

But the girls would not listen to me.

The strikers from the other shop began to picket our place, appealing to the workers for help. The boss placed a few policemen to guard the doors and protect us from "those dangerous people." With contempt I chased a policeman away from me, when he took me under his arm to protect me as a picket approached me on my way out from the elevator.

"Look out, little girl, they will hurt you," he said.

"I shall call for you when I need you," I replied.

"Well, well, I'm here to keep order."

The pickets did not know how hard I was trying to get our people to join them in their strike. Their eyes would follow me with hatred as they followed all the others, who did not care to help them. The boss and designer learned that I tried to appeal to the sample-makers. They did not say anything to me, but their angry looks and the difference in their treatment told me what I might expect.

It was on a Friday at lunch-time. We had only half an hour for lunch and usually ate inside. I had to go down to the union office on the request of the manager. When I had my coat and hat on, the boss came over to me and asked where I was going. I told him that I had n't any lunch and was going down to a restaurant. Suspecting that I would be watched, I went into a restaurant, but only to walk through it and out through another door. At the union I had a talk with the manager and got some instructions from him what to do. When I came back to the shop, I was not admitted. Without any explanation I was given my pay for a full week and told to go.

The strikers, after being two weeks on strike, returned to work with bowed heads; the more active girls who organized the strike were not taken back.

It was then the end of November. Again, I tasted the bitterness of the slack season, now worse than ever, for we were two people — to the last penny I had to provide for my brother.

The room I stayed in was dreadful. When I worked, I was home so seldom that I did not mind so much. But when I was out of work and home most of the time, I realized the surroundings I was in. There were five rooms in the house. Two bedrooms, a front room, dining-room, and kitchen. Husband, wife, and two children slept in one bedroom, two of their sisters slept in the dining-room, two girl boarders slept in the front room, and a boy slept in the kitchen. I and my brother slept in the last bedroom. While to me the house seemed worse than hell, the people in the house thought it not so bad, for in all the block, everybody kept at least four or five boarders, in addition to their own big families — and they were no exceptions.

Bedbugs were everywhere, not only in the beds, — they were even in the closets with the clothes, on my bookcases with the books.

Oh, how miserably those days passed! Sometimes I would clean my room all day long, clean, clean, but the bugs would come in from the next room and I could never rid myself of them. The air from so many people in the house was so thick that I would have to hold my breath while passing at night to my room. The result of that environment was a nasal catarrh which has been with me ever since.

I had to run away from there if I valued my health, but I could not move out until I found work.

From home I would run away to the office of the union, where I would spend most of the day. There I met hundreds of new girls each day, hundreds of starved faces crying for help, crying for justice. When the day's work would be over, I would sit and talk to the managers. It gave me much pleasure to spend my time with them. Their conversations were so interesting, so refreshing. I was not the only one to enjoy their warm friendship. I was one of them, one of the thousands for whom their hearts beat with love and devotion.

For two weeks I chased the city, until I found a job, a union shop. Here again I met with the same experience as in my first union shop in slack time. The boss lowered the prices and the workers refused to accept the low prices. The same quarrelling, the same bargaining as in my other shops.

On the price committee were two girls, both of them experienced workers, who had been in the trade about twelve years and could judge very well the right price for a garment. One of them — Sophie was her name — would fight for a price more than the other. She was a girl of twenty-seven years. Her pronunciation was a little peculiar. She pronounced *sh* as *s* and *s* she pronounced *sh;* her *ch* came out *ts*. The foreman desired so much to get rid of her on the price committee that he would try to tease and cheapen her before the girls. He would imitate her pronunciation at every opportunity —

"Hey, Shophie, I wis' that you would get married; you are too old to shettle prices."

"Shophie, don't eat tsocolate, you will spoil your old teeth."

That poor girl swallowed the insults without saying a word.

What provoked me most was that the girls for whom she fought would burst into giggling at the foreman's stupid jokes.

The foreman was very kind to me the first days;

he found pleasure in calling me "little daughter," although he was too young to be my father.

My machine, which was an old one, was impossible to work on, and he promised to change it for a better one. On Monday of the second week a few new machines were placed and I got one of the new ones. They were Wilcox and Gibbs machines, much quicker than the others, but even on those we could make very little at the prices that were paid, and one morning we stopped work. The boss called for a clerk from the union, and when the latter came we explained to him that we refused to make up the work because the boss did not pay a satisfactory price. Somehow, with the help of the clerk, the prices were adjusted and we began work again. But instead of giving the settled prices to his people, he sent the work outside claiming that he could get it done cheaper. We learned the very same day that the work was sent up to the eleventh floor in the same building. It was also a union shop and our boss did not get his work any cheaper, but he simply wanted to punish us. In the evening, we had a meeting to talk things over. I urged the girls not to compromise on prices because that might injure the workers in the other shops as well as ourselves. A committee of two was selected to watch where the work was sent out so that we might prevent it.

The next morning when I stood near the counter,

waiting for work, the foreman asked me, "Are you also mixing in politics, little daughter?"

As through magic he seemed to know what had been done at the meeting, and after that I was no more "little daughter." It was, "Miss, you spoiled that yoke. Miss, you made a mistake in the size. Hey, miss, the stitches are too big." Everything suddenly went wrong with my work. The aggravation I had through the foreman that day caused me such a terrible headache that at four o'clock I had to go home and lie down.

CHAPTER XIII

AT home, to my great surprise, I found the table in my room set with fruit, corned beef, ham, and many other good things. At the table sat my brother and another young man. They both jumped up, as if taken unawares. In the young fellow I recognized my brother's pal from home. I was surprised to find him here. My brother called me out of the room to explain: —

"Looking around for work, to-day, I found him on the street. We were both surprised to see each other. He was looking for work also. He has been out of work for a long time and he gave up his room, two days ago, not having any money to pay his rent. He slept in the park last night. I was so broken-hearted by his story that I forgot to think that we ourselves had no money. The dollar you gave me for car-fare, I spent for all that food. I purposely bought a lot of things to make him think that we had enough. He must be starved. He did not want to come up; he thought that you would not want me to spend so much money when I had no work; but I assured him that you were working in the shop and would not know it. And even if you did know, you would not be against it, would you, dear?" he ended in a begging tone.

"Of course, I would not, but why did you buy so much? There is enough food for six people. Now you will have no car-fare, how are you going to look for a job?"

"Oh, it's all right, I'll walk. I am strong enough to walk for a week," he said, stretching out his muscles to show me his strength.

Poor boy, what a young, self-sacrificing thing! In order to comfort his friend, he spent all the money he had. I knew it was impossible for my brother to walk. He had to inquire about work in different places both up and down town, so that I had to give him another dollar and that meant to economize still further in our food. But I admired his generosity. Trying to smile, I entered the room, sat at the table with them, and tried to make them forget their troubles. I could not eat, but with delight I watched both of them consuming the food with great appetites. Not much was left when they had finished. As the boy had no room, I told them I would go and stay overnight with Clara, so that he could have my bed. I also gave them ten cents for a moving-picture show.

I tried to rest, but I was in a very nervous condition, and could not fall asleep. I felt tired and displeased with everything. "What is to-morrow?" I asked myself — the same trouble in the shop with no hope in the future, slack season, starvation, — oh, how terrible, how monotonous, life continues!

When the clock struck seven, I got up. I had a ticket for the opera that evening and did not want to miss it.

My friend Clara accompanied me to the opera house. On the last bench of the family circle, so high that the people on the stage looked like dwarfs, we sat silently waiting for the music to start. Clara made several attempts to start a conversation, but I tried to avoid it; it was hard for me to talk. I was tired of telling the same old stories over and over again.

"Take it easy, take it easy, kiddo," Clara tried to comfort me.

"Oh, no, Clara, you are wrong, wrong; did people not take life so easily, we would have a much better world than we have now," I argued.

"I often think that you are a mystery to me, Lisa. I cannot imagine that you — so full of life — should be so pessimistic. Now you jump, sing, and laugh like a careless child. Then your eyes fill with sadness, your head drops as if all the world lay heavy on your shoulders."

"Yes, Clara, it is true. Just because I am full of life, I am pessimistic. Like a fish without water, I am wriggling in this world without happiness. Clara, where is the happiness of our youth? Where is it?" I whispered in agony. "I want joy, I am young, I am entitled to it, I do not want to content myself with a dry, sucked-out bone that is thrown to me. I want it all — life in its full thickness! I want my roses, I have had enough thorns. I cannot stand it any longer, I am tired of it, tired of everything."

The music started. I was all transformed into attention. I bathed my soul in the wonderful sounds of the music, trying to wash off the heavy melancholy that possessed me, gnawing, gnawing, at my heart and soul.

He who has once heard that opera surely remembers the sweet music and beautiful words of the aria from the third act of "La Tosca": —

"When the stars were brightly shining
And faint perfume the air pervaded,
Creaked the gate of the garden,
And a footstep its precincts invaded.
'T was hers, the fragrant creature,
In her soft arms she clasped me,
With sweetest kisses, tenderest caresses,
A thing of beauty, matchless symmetry and feature,
My dream of love is now dispelled forever.
I lived uncaring,
And now I die despairing!
Yet ne'er was life so dear to me, no, never." [1]

Thousands of angels began dancing in the air around me when Caruso began the aria.

Now slowly and melodiously, now loudly, — thundering with despair, — now mournfully, with heart-breaking, thrilling sobs, — the music sobbing quietly in accord.

[1] English translation by W. B. Kingston.

How I wished that it would never end! To sit there, to listen with bated breath to the heavenly sounds, to drink, drink those delicious melodies and never again return to miserable reality!

On our way home I was very silent. I thought of the successful artists of whose early life I had read. Who knows, perhaps if I could only have a chance to show my abilities (I had a good soprano voice) — but I immediately caught myself up in that daring thought.

But I am very emotional. Many people at home in Russia had advised me to select a stage career. I myself had the strongest wish to become an actress, but my parents would not listen to it — they had a very bad opinion of an actress, they saw no art in it.

Here in New York I had often thought of it, but I was afraid to try, for I knew no one who could give me an introduction to any one interested in the stage. And not knowing the English language, I could not succeed in trying all alone without anybody's help.

I lay in bed awake, my brains puzzled with questions. The condition of life in which I was placed enchained me and drove me into a frenzy. I could not stand it. I must get away from such a life — but how? What can I do in order to better my economic condition, and make my life more attractive, fill it with more interest?

I can do nothing but make waists and that can give me just enough to lead a miserable life. With the exception of those who are helped out by their parents, all the workers in our industry and also in many others live in terrible surroundings. Many of them not only support themselves, but have to support their parents or brothers or sisters.

With a still worse headache, I awoke the next morning. Clara advised me to stay home until my headache was better, but I could not afford to do that and I went to work. Thousands of people were automatically pushing through the streets to their shops. At the square on Fourteenth Street, the people would flow in from all the streets into the small path, and, like quiet waves, one crowd would flow after the other. It was a great big army, an army of young girls, middle-aged mothers, young fellows, and old fathers. With rayless eyes, with drooping heads, they walked. In vain the young girls tried to cover with paint and powder their faded-before-its-time beauty; their movements were quick but automatic.

Like in a funeral procession, I walked among them — I saw before me an army of mourners — I saw an army of convicts, people who were sentenced to eternal poverty, to eternal misery.

"Will they ever raise their heads, will they ever stand up and throw off those who sit on their backs?" I thought.

"If the workers would only realize their strength and use it jointly, how quickly they could revolutionize the world!"

These words, once said by one of the managers of our union, still rang in my ears.

"Yes," I thought, "if they would only realize, what a better world they could create!"

When I entered the shop, I found my new machine taken away and the old broken one in its place. I went over to see the foreman and asked him the reason for that.

He said, "A good worker can work on any machine."

"But my machine is a broken one, it breaks the threads every other second and it is difficult to make a straight stitch," I argued.

"What would you do if I had not brought in any new machines at all?"

"But you brought new machines, because it was impossible to work with the old ones," I said.

"Now, don't give me any arguments. I see that you are looking for trouble. I have no other machine for you. Don't bother me."

I tried the machine again, but it would not work, and I spent all morning without making a stitch.

It was evident that the foreman wanted to rid himself of me, because I had advised the girls to stand up for their rights.

At lunch-time the chairlady went downstairs

with me. I was too upset to think of eating, so we took a walk. She expressed her sympathy and wanted to go to the union and complain, but I would not let her. I did not like to complain about myself. Besides, the boss could have a good argument by stating that he had no other machine, that the new machine was sent away because he did not like it. He could give all sorts of arguments about the machine and I did not want our union clerk to bother in vain.

What was I to do? To go back to the shop meant sitting near the machine, throwing time away. To go home meant still worse. And the day was such a glorious one! It was one of those beautiful early December days when the air is so frosty and fresh. Automobiles were rushing up and down Fifth Avenue, carrying people with happy, self-contented faces.

"Who are those people? How and where do they get those expensive autos, those warm furs, and time enough to enjoy the midday ride? Are they working for it? If so, where and how? If I work so hard and get just mere bread, a filthy home, and a poor thin coat, how hard must they work to get those costly furs and those beautiful clothes?"

I went back to the shop, but could not work. The winter's sun shone through the window, and its rays were so soothing.

"Out, out! Oh, how beautiful it is outdoors!

Here the people sit rushing their machines to make a few more cents, a few more cents to add to their small earnings; they do not have time to glance at the beautiful sun; they do not notice its alluring call. Oh, out, out to the park, — play with the snowballs, run in the snow, skate on the ice, — out, out, to laugh carelessly, to play freely, to think clearly, to forget the misery! Oh, out, out!"

At last, with great effort, I had my bundle of work finished. As soon as I started to work on a new bundle, I had my first bundle brought back to me to be fixed. The foreman did not like the way I had made it up. I saw nothing wrong with it but if any one wishes to find fault it could be found with the best sample.

After I had fixed it, he did not like the way I had fixed it. I saw no way to please him. The chairlady had an argument with him about it. She was enraged with his action, but he cared little. I knew I could complain to the union, but I also knew that if the foreman had made up his mind to get rid of me, I would have to complain every day.

Yes, he handled me as he pleased; my weakness against him pained me.

I sat by the machine exhausted and upset. "What was I to do?" My head still ached, my thoughts began to mingle — the shop, the foreman with his arguments, the opera of last night, my brother, his pal — everything danced before me in dark confusion. I grew weaker and weaker and felt that I was breaking down.

Not to show my weakness I stood up, straightened myself quickly, took my coat and left. For a long time I wandered around the streets, resting in the squares, until I went to Clara. With her I always felt better. Late that night, I returned home. My brother, thinking I was not coming, had his friend with him again. That poor boy immediately sprang up to go away, but I would not let him. Together with my brother he slept in a narrow single bed while I slept in the other.

The next afternoon I went to the union office. Mr. Baroff, the manager, was surprised to see me in the middle of the day.

"What happened? Are you not working?"

"I left because I did not like the place," I answered.

He looked at me. I suppose he understood my downhearted mood, for he did not question me any more. He only said: "I do not think that you will find any work until January. It is useless to look for work now. You had better stay home and rest until the busy season begins."

I looked at him. Did he really mean what he said or was he joking?

He guessed my thoughts, for he immediately explained to me: —

"My dear girl, you must be more sensible, and

more trustful of people of my age. When I asked you to accept the money I offered you" (he once offered me a loan, but I had refused to accept it), "I did not mean to give it to you. I only wanted to help you out until you and your brother find good jobs and could repay me. You are not the only one to whom I lend money. I have not much, but little as I have, I will gladly help you until you begin to work, and then you will repay me. I know you will."

I sat on the chair deadly pale. It was the second time that he had offered me money. He simply begged me to accept it, assuring me that he, also, had once been in need and his friends had helped him until he was able to repay.

But I had never borrowed any money from a man. I felt insulted when a man offered to make me a loan. My friend Clara was the only person from whom I ever took money and that money was already repaid.

"After all, he is only a good friend to me; he is so different from other men. Why not accept the money for a time? I will be able to return it as I did Clara's," I thought.

"But if I am not able to repay, if I secure a job and am not able to make enough to pay my debt, what will I do then? Remain in debt? Oh, no, no, — " I did not accept the loan.

Coming home that night, I had an argument with

the mistress of the house. She demanded pay for the two nights the boy spent with us. That was the limit for me. The boy slept in our room. My brother shared his bed with him. Nothing of hers was touched, not even a special sheet, and she wanted to be paid just because the room was in her house. Of course, I refused, for I had not the money to pay.

"I also want an extra quarter for the additional gas that you used this month. I think that I could get nine dollars for two people in this room instead of eight," she added.

"Well, all right; you are at liberty to rent this room for as much as you can get. We will move next month," I replied.

I was provoked at her greed, but she was no exception. In almost every house where I had had a room, except the coöperative house, the landlady did not like to see me burn gas after ten o'clock in the evening.

CHAPTER XIV

NOW that I was forced to move, what was I to do?

Accept the money or not accept it? A job I would not find until the season started. It was five or six weeks more to wait. I had no more than three dollars to end the week. How was I to begin the next week? How? How?

I felt that the nervous strain was weakening me, that my health would surely break down if my present circumstances did not change. If not for myself, for my brother I had to borrow money, for I felt responsible for his sufferings. Seeing no other way of helping myself, I at last accepted the loan, which was sufficient for us to live on, by being very economical, during the next five weeks. I decided to move uptown where rent is cheaper and the surrounding air is purer.

It was queer how I began to avoid meeting Mr. Baroff after I accepted his loan. Formerly I had been glad to meet him often, to have our talks which never ended. Now, I tried to avoid him, much to his amazement. He did not know what had happened to me. I was of the opinion that friendship ceases as soon as one tries to profit by a friend's kindness. I imagined that by the acceptance of the loan, I had broken the bonds of our friendship which I had valued so much. Oh, how regretful and hurt I often felt when I thought of it! But I could not prevent it. I took the money; I had to accept it whether it was right or wrong.

My brother could not stay with me uptown, for he had to look for work in the downtown sections, so I found for him a place to board at three dollars a week on Avenue B. For myself, I found a room on 113th Street, near Central Park, for five dollars a month, which was as big, or as small, as the room I had downtown. For one person, it was all right. The room, at least, was much cleaner and there were only two people in the house besides me.

With money to live on for the next few weeks, I tried to rest and be comfortable. Next to my house, in a three-room apartment, lived a young couple, friends of mine, with whom I spent a great deal of my time. The wife kept house and took up a course in school-teaching, for she did not believe in a woman's dependence on her husband, and she expected to become a school-teacher in order that she might be self-supporting. I have seldom known such a happy family among the people I have met. The harmony of ideas, the love and devotion that this couple showed to each other, attracted me greatly, and I always felt happy to spend my time with them.

Attending once a lecture at the Francisco Ferrer Centre I met a Canadian lady who had given me a few lessons in English when I was in Toronto, Canada. We were both surprised to see each other in such a radical institution as the Modern School. I had first met her in a settlement where she taught English to foreigners. Her appearance and her kindness made me think that she was one of the missionaries of which Toronto is so full. I was almost sure that she was a missionary until that evening when I met her at the Modern School. She was very glad to see me there, and badly as I spoke even then, she could understand me much better than the last time I had seen her.

We became interested in each other and I gladly accepted her invitation to dinner. She lived in a small apartment on East 79th Street. The cosy, neatly furnished rooms, her own household, seemed to me a paradise in comparison with my own small room, where there was nothing but a bed, a chair, and a table. She had her own dishes, her own linen, her own furniture, everything of her own. She did as she pleased and when she pleased, while I, since I had left my parents in Russia, had had almost nothing of my own.

"How nice and pleasant it feels to have an apartment of your own with everything to please one's self," I thought. "But as girls in my circumstances can get their own apartment only as an appendage to a husband, and as some of us do not want or cannot get one, they consequently cannot have an apartment for themselves."

After dinner we began to tell each other about our lives. I told her all about myself since I left Toronto and she told me her experiences. She was very much interested in the labor movement. In 1913, when the general strike broke out in the needle trade, she came over from Toronto and helped organize the wrapper and kimono workers. When the strike was over, she was very weak and took a trip to England. Now she was back again working for the suffrage movement.

Before I left she asked me to come to visit her often. I promised to do so.

CHAPTER XV

IN the middle of January I at last found a job in a union shop of about two hundred workers. The chairlady was a very gentle, sympathetic person. She had worked in that shop for two years and was popular with the workers, but there was one fault with her: she was too autocratic in her actions. Among the hundred and fifty girls there were about fifteen or twenty intelligent, active union members who were interested in the good and welfare of the shop. But she would consult no one about the shop business; she asked no one's opinion and did everything according to her own judgment. With the best intentions she could not take care of so many people, when, besides representing the workers, she had to earn her living. The boss selected a few favorites to whom he gave the best and most work, thus securing them as his supporters. It is quite customary for every employer, whether good or bad, to have some favorites in the shop whom he uses against their fellow-workers. If any dispute arises in the shop, they are always on the side of the boss. He also supplied the chairlady with a better share of the work so as to distract her attention from the unequal division of work. The chairlady in her anxiety to make up for lost time accepted the larger portion of work, but failed to see how displeasing it was to the other workers, arousing their jealousy and often distrust toward her.

Another and very important thing neglected was organizing the workers as true, conscious union members. The understanding of unionism by most of the girls was limited to paying dues, which often they tried to avoid; also not scabbing in time of a strike. They needed to be educated and enlightened as to the cause of unity. If the chairlady had only been willing to coöperate with the few active girls in the shop, this might have been accomplished; alone she worked very hard and could not attend to everything.

On the whole, it was a good shop. Despite its many faults it was much better than the many other shops where I worked before and after. It was very busy, the styles were simple that season, the prices fair, and the workers earned fair wages.

I felt pleased to find a shop with an intelligent chairlady. I was tired out; I longed for a place where I could work uninterruptedly, at least for a season, and pay off my debt. In this new shop of mine my union activity was not essential, so I could sit quietly and work. And I was quiet. Among the many girls I was noticed very little. The fourth week my eyes began to bother me a great deal. My machine happened to be in a very dark corner, and I had to work by gas-light all day. My eyes first became impaired in that historic association shop which I tried to organize. Now, as soon as I worked by gas-light, my eyes would become inflamed and cause me headaches. I asked the boss to allow me to change my machine. He had two empty machines in front near the windows — but he refused. Why did he refuse? What difference would it make to him if he had given me the empty machine near the window? I did not know. My eyes became worse from day to day. My headaches were more frequent, causing me heavy nightmares night after night. One evening at home I was terrified when I saw my eyes in the mirror — they were bloodshot. Visions of blindness crowded my mind.

"Goodness!" I cried in fear. "Better dead than sightless!" I lay in bed, my imagination picturing the horror of blindness. I closed my smarting eyelids, and in the darkness I began to ponder, climbing high, high over something smooth, but suddenly fell back. What was it? I wanted to open my eyes, but I could not, I could not separate my eyelids. I was blind, blind already, and from all around pitiful voices sounded: "Make way for her, make way for the poor cripple." They all pitied me, they took care of me, but I was too heavy a burden, and finally they left me alone. And in this forever-dark-to-me world, I am groping my way, singing and begging — pennies flying into my outstretched hands. My former bosses meet me, they laugh, they scoff with revenge, and with a sneer wave their hand.

"Ha! ha! ha! that is what you get for your union and your foolish sentimentality for your fellow-workers."

"You made me go out of business when I was so kind and gave you all chances for your future advancement. I wanted to give you two helpers through whom you could make money besides your earnings, — and I wanted to make you my fore-lady."

"And I — I — Don't you remember me? Don't you remember that Saturday when we were alone in the office and you ran away leaving your pay in my hands? Ha! ha! ha! will you run away now? Can you see where? You may meet some one worse than I. Ha! ha! ha! — come over here. Sing for me, — no, dance for me, — show your grace now. Come on — a nickel a dance. Dance before me as Salome before Herod the king. Ha! ha! ha!"

I was driven to dance, was made a laughing-stock. "Livelier! Livelier!" they shouted from all around. And livelier I danced, I sang, I jumped, until my head felt giddy, my senses began to twirl, my strength failed me, and I dropped down. I screamed and — awoke on the floor.

In the silent darkness the shadows of that senseless, mad dream boldly stood out, growing longer and longer, but I was not blind. I saw all, I saw everything in its ugly vividness. Each *tick-tock* of the clock made me thrill with terror. Each hour lengthened itself out like a century. Would the morning never come? It seemed as if there was no end to that frightful night.

In the morning, instead of going to work, I went to look for another job. I valued my eyesight too much to risk it further, and I found a place with enough daylight.

It was an association shop. The firm manufactured a common line of cotton dresses. Workers were hired by the week. Our union had no minimum wage for week operators, for it demanded the piece-work system. The association was supposed to enforce that system in all its shops, but many manufacturers did not carry out the demand, giving different reasons for their failure to do so. While the piece-price in a union shop was fixed by the workers and the boss, the weekly price was always fixed by either the foreman or boss. It was up to the workers to remain for the price offered or to look for a better job. Workers were often very much wronged by the week-work system.

When I asked for my price, in a few days, I was offered nine dollars. That sounded like a joke.

I showed the foreman my pay envelope from

the previous week's earnings, which amounted to $15.45.

"Why did you leave that job?"

"Because my machine was in a dark place and the artificial light had hurt my eyes."

"Well, in here you have a good light place; is it not worth while to stay here for less?"

"For less, but not for so much less. Must I pay you six dollars a week just for getting a machine in a light place?" I asked angrily.

"My dear little girl, who says you must? Nobody is keeping you here."

I left that place. I would not work for nine dollars when I knew I was worth fifteen.

As I had left some unfinished work in my old shop, I returned to finish and get my pay. The forelady was glad to see me back.

"I hope you do not desert us any more," she said, as she gave me my bundle.

"I will not, if I get a machine by the window," I answered, explaining why I had left the shop.

Through her and also through help of the chairlady I got a machine near the window, hoping that nothing else would happen, for I liked that shop.

Had my brother found work I could have allowed myself to live a little better, for in comparison with my former earnings I made more now. But to support my brother and pay my debts I had not enough for myself. I heard that the seasons in my shop are always short, and if I had not any money saved up for the dull season I should have to live through the same life as in the former slack seasons. I shuddered at those thoughts. I had lived through three horrid dull seasons and I felt that physically I could not endure any further strain.

My brother worried me terribly. Not being able to find work, he was much discouraged and would always walk around downcast. Tears were always in his eyes when I brought him money to pay up his board. "To think that such a delicate girl as you should have to work so hard to support me — such a strong big boy with iron muscles as mine are!" he would often say. I could do naught but comfort him.

Once when I came to visit him (I visited him twice a week) I found him in bed with a terrible toothache. In vain did he try to hide his agonies.

"It is nothing, sister, it will pass soon, it's only a light toothache." He tried to comfort me, setting his teeth together from pain.

"Will you go over to the dentist?" I asked him.

"Oh, no, no! I do not need any dentist, I assure you."

His head was warm, his eyes burned with fever. He must have caught a cold. He broke my heart as I looked at him. "What if he gets sick!" I was thrilled by that thought. "Oh, no, he would not, he must not!"

Sitting at his bedside my eyes were fixed at the floor. I noticed his shoes. I picked them up. Both soles were rubbed out and wide open. He did not dare to ask me for extra money to have his shoes repaired. "My fault, my fault! How did I neglect to ask him if his shoes were in order? Now if he gets sick, it is mine whose fault it'll be!"

I took his shoes and immediately went down to have them repaired.

When I came up again he asked me smilingly, "Will you be so nice and show me your shoes; are they in perfect order?"

"Why, sure they are," I answered, raising my foot to show them to him, when I first learned that mine were also open. How I walked around not knowing that my shoe-soles were open, I do not know. "I intend to buy new ones, so that I thought they were not worth while fixing," I stammered.

Indeed, it was not worth while fixing it, the shoemaker told me when I brought it down to him next Sunday to be repaired. (I could not spare my shoes in the middle of the week.) So for a long time I wore a pair of old rubbers to cover my soles. In wet or dry weather I always had them on.

At home that evening I sank in thoughts of myself. Two years in America! Two years in the golden country! What had I accomplished? — a weak stomach, headaches every other day, a pale face, inflamed eyes, and my nose — my nose also began to complain. It wanted a doctor and I could not afford to pay for one. To a dispensary I had no time to go and I would not, even if I had time. One dollar made a world of differences. For a dollar the doctor would gently open the door for the patient, would offer a thousand smiles, take his time, and examine the patient thoroughly. In the dispensary sometimes one had to waste all day to get his turn, and when at last the chance came, the patient would be treated so gruffly he would feel as though he had not come to the doctor for advice but to spoil his good moods.

If my mother could only know, if she could *only* know! But never should she know! It is enough for her, when she had to part with us. As she wrote once to me: "Another child gone, another wound in mother's heart! Oh, where are my children, my little birds? Was mother's nest too small for them? Oh, if only I were a free bird now, if only I had wings. I would fly, fly, through night and day, through storm and sunshine, through oceans and forests only to have a look at you, my children, who left mother to find a better life, to build better nests. For so many years I struggled. In the long, cold, stormy winter nights, I watched over you, cherished you. With my tears and prayers to God I obtained your lives when death stood many a time at your bedside, waiting for mother to give you up. Never did I give you up. You were my pride, you were my light in the dark life of my struggle against poverty. And you gave up mother so easily! You left your home with no regret! You left your mother to her tears! Oh, where are you now? Are you happy, are you warm, are you fed? If I could only embrace you once more, feel you near my wounded heart! Other people have the pleasure to hear you talk, to hear you laugh, to hear you sing! Are you still singing, my little daughter, or is your voice forgotten under the heavy burden of the new life?"

That letter made me hysterical for a few hours when I received it, and long afterwards, whenever I re-read it, I could not keep from crying. There is so much tragedy in each word of that letter. The tragedy of all the Jewish mothers whose children escape from where they suffer, from Russian brutality, from Galician poverty. Youth does not want to bow its head as its parents did, nor stand for so much misery — oh, so much! Youth wants life, happiness. In the hunt for a better, freer life, Youth parts with its dear parents: parts full of hope to be reunited in a better land, in better circumstances. But more often the hopes are crushed, the lives are broken. Not all are able to reunite, and they remain parted far, far away from one another. The eternal anxiety for one another tears the heart and soul to pieces. Neither the children in America nor their parents abroad can ever be happy when they are torn apart.

"Never should she know!" I repeated to myself, and to comfort her I immediately sat down to write a letter: —

"*Much beloved Mother:* — To begin with I want to inform you that I am in perfect health and happiness, wishing to hear the same from you."

Here I stopped. "Wishing to hear the same from you!" Alas, I surely do not wish to curse my mother! I tore up the letter. But what shall I tell her? What shall I write to her about? I took another sheet.

"*My best of best Mothers:* — With delight I read your last letter. I was so happy to learn that everything at home is in order. Please, mother, don't cry. It worries me terribly. We are not dead, we are alive. We'll try our very best to have you all with us in the nearest future. Oh, how happy I shall be when I have you all with us! Sorrow will be forgotten and the guardian angels will spread their wings over us and watch our happiness, and never, never again will we part! Tell the children that I will answer their letters some other time. Nathan's poem, which he dedicated to me, is very hearty, but I don't like his grammar in it. This was always his weak point. Tell him to pay more attention to the Russian grammar. You know, mother, I do think that he is an able little fellow.

He is only sixteen now, and if he has good opportunities he will be successful.

"With pride you tell me, mother, that little Eva is my double — that physically and mentally she resembles me. I want to hope that she should be much better than I am and more successful. How is Sarah? Is she diligent in her studies? Is Dora stronger now than she was? Have you any letters from Israel, or does he write only when he needs money? Poor fellow, two more years he must spend in the military service.[1]

"Please, mother, send me his address. I want to write a letter to him. About us you should not worry. We are all right.

"My best regards to all the children and father, — to him I will write to-morrow. I have so much to tell him! Our discussions by correspondence were stopped for quite a long time, and I want to begin again. Is he still working so hard? Mother dear, take care of yourself, father and the children.

"With love for everybody,

"LISA."

I was up very early the next morning. After having my light breakfast, which always consisted of a glass of milk, I went to work. It was too early

[1] He is compelled to serve a country which deprived him of all possible liberty, of human rights. At present, when I write these lines, he is back home with a wounded leg.

to go to the shop, so I turned in to the park for a short while. With deep, hungry breath I drank the frozen air which was so refreshing.

I watched the little frozen lake surrounded by naked trees covered with sleet, and it seemed to remind me of homeless, poorly clad, lonely old women shivering with cold.

The high rocks majestically stood out of the white snow that covered the ground. For a while there came back to me those bygone days when as children we would steal out from the classroom and run off to turn somersaults and stretch on the snow, making human-like figures; how often would we skate and play with snowballs late into the evening, returning home with glowing faces! Happy but exhausted we would fall on our beds, and with our clothes on sleep the night right through. Even in the later years, when the happy carelessness was gone with our childhood, when life made us more thoughtful — even then the winter had its charms for us. We would go off in groups, exploring the snow-clad woods and groves, enjoying the frosty but romantic moonlight. Here this picturesque park was deserted. Hundreds of people were passing by, and what a pity they paid no attention to it — they hurried anxiously to the near-by subway for an earlier train, to be in time for work.

In this hurry-up, made world, they had no time to look around them — in this world of efficiency they were blinded to all natural beauty. In this world of freedom they were made to work only — work or starve, nay, work and starve. Human beings were turned into machine value, their strength was turned into dollars. This new world full of riches turned life into gray prose, made people a slave to the dollar — even art seems to be measured in the terms of money.

A chill ran through my body. Was it the realization of such a world, or was I so meagrely clad for such a frosty morning — I was recalled to my duties — to work, work and turn my work into dollars.

At half-past seven I took the subway train downtown. The trains in the mornings and evenings were over-packed. The people were pressed together like sardines in a tin box. It was very hard to breathe. I always tried to stand close to the door with my face turned away from people, for the worst kinds of diseases could easily be contracted, being so close to other people's breathing. Girls sometimes fainted in those crowded cars from the thick air. I always got headaches travelling in the subways. In Russia no more passengers than seats are allowed. Here in free America the people are free to choke themselves with the suffocating subway air. They are thrown together like cattle and carried down to the industrial market. From the people's nickels the company's millions grow like weeds, and they could have enough cars to prevent such dangerous crowding, if only they cared enough for public welfare.

I was the first one in the shop that morning. The workers usually filled up the place between a quarter after eight and nine o'clock. With great diligence I began to work. Oh, if I could only have work enough for day and evening! I would willingly work evenings, too, could I only get the work. I had to earn enough for myself, for doctor's bills; I had to save up some money in order to bring my parents over here. Perhaps if we could be together, we would not suffer so much. If we — the older children — could not succeed, we could at least try for the younger ones — we could help them so as to keep them out of the miserable factory life.

How I liked the work that day! I was thankful to the boss, to the forelady, even to the girl who gave out the work. My work as if by magic went through my hands. I completed bundle after bundle without any interruption. For lunch I only spent ten cents instead of my regular fifteen cents. I wanted to save from whatever I could. For the first time I made four dollars and fifty cents in that day, but it was also the last, for I never made that much in the shop again. I was so happy. "What if I would make four dollars and a half every day!" I began to calculate — that would make twenty-four dollars a week. "Oh, it would be a fortune!"

thought I, forgetting to think of my delicate health that did not even stand for one day of such hard work. I did not belong to the very quick workers. I was one of the average, and the highest I ever made in a week was eighteen dollars. After that day's work I had to attend a meeting of the organization committee of our union. I was a member of the organization committee and helped in organizing the non-union shops.

During the year 1913–14 a number of manufacturers broke away from the Manufacturers' Association and restored their shops to the former conditions. It only happened in those shops where the people were badly unionized. They were weaklings, and the bosses saw their chances to break with the union in order to have their own ways with the workers. Those open shops began to increase and some of the workers who protested against breaking with the union, were thrown out of the shops. The same happened with some non-protocol union shops. The organization committee — consisting of an organizer, a few executive board members, and members of our union — tried to get those shops unionized again, for we saw great danger if we let those open shops exist. Without the control of the union the standards would become lower and lower, and the low standards in the open shops would certainly injure the higher standards in the union shops.

We were divided into committees of two or three members, and each committee was assigned every other day to a shop. In the morning between seven and eight and in the evening between five-thirty and six-thirty, we would come over to the door of the open shop and distribute circulars. The circulars were printed in Yiddish, English, and Italian, with an appeal to the people to get organized. But we made very slow progress, for only a small number of our union members were willing to give their time and energy for organization work. We needed many people to do the work and did not get them.

I was assigned to go out early next morning with some circulars. From the meeting I ran over to see my brother. He felt a little better. I came home at eleven in the evening. I felt very tired and sleepy. Being afraid to eat before bedtime, I went to sleep without my supper. In the morning I could hardly get up. I must have exhausted myself too much the day before. With great effort I dressed myself and went downtown with the circulars. It was an extremely cold day and I stood outside for an hour distributing the circulars and trying to speak to the people — to appeal to them. My thin short coat and my torn shoes were of very little protection against the frost. I stood freezing patiently. When I went to work at half-past eight I nearly fainted from weakness, and before long my strength failed me and I had to go home and rest. So for making four and a half dollars in one day I had to pay with another day. I lay in bed blaming myself for my weakness. Alas, I can't afford to be sick in the height of the season. But in order to keep up my health, I realized that I must feed myself better, have warm clothes, and enough sleep. But how am I to get enough money for all that? Oh, that money problem! How much longer will that occupy my mind? How much longer will that last? I'm so sick of it! Work, work! Struggle, struggle! and not even enough from hand to mouth! No time for reading, no money for recreation! Nothing but work, worry, worry and work. How shall I get rid of the shop — that free prison? I shall be choked by its surroundings if I stay there any longer. I can't, I can't bear a life full of emptiness! How happy are those who can fight patiently! My patience is broken! With my body and soul I protest against such a life! And I can do nothing to change it. How weak I am! How shamefully weak!

CHAPTER XVI

FROM that day on I ceased to do my work regularly. My headaches and depressed moods would keep me in bed too often. I would come into the shop at ten in the mornings, sometimes stop in the afternoon, or leave the shop at five o'clock instead of six. I very seldom put in a full day's work. The boss was very much displeased to see me coming at such irregular hours. He warned me he would send me away if I did not come in time, for he could not afford to keep a machine waiting for me even for a few hours. I knew he would do it and tried to come in time, but I worked very slowly. I would sometimes take a bundle of work, and taking it apart never see or realize what I was doing; the different parts of the work would mingle before my eyes and it would take me a long time to distinguish one part from the other. The forelady would often ask — "*Hundred and twelve,* what happened to you?" (We were called by numbers in most of the shops.) "You are giving out too little work lately." I tried my best, but could not help being slow. My mind was upset, and very often, when I tried to absorb myself in the work, and press the foot of my machine to make it run faster, I would not notice that my foot had stopped pressing and the machine was not going until a neighbor would awake me with a joke. "How do the people look like on Mars?" I would then shake myself and resume work.

In my depression I sought quietness and would spend the most of my time alone in my little room.

My new friend Alice was the only one whom I visited frequently. With her I often discussed my situation. She agreed that I must leave the shop, for it was no place for me. The shop under the present conditions is good for no human being to work in. She also agreed that I must study English, before I could do anything else.

Her desire was for me to become a labor organizer. Myself, I was very enthusiastic for organizing work, but I feared that I could never make a good speaker, which I thought was necessary for an organizer.

Free as I felt when I spoke at shop meetings, or among the girls at work, I would not feel free on the public platform. It was hard to decide. The first thing to do was to conquer the language, then study the labor questions, the social evils of the present and past centuries, before I had a right to think of becoming an organizer. But how was I to study? I was so tired after a day's work that my brain was too dull for study. And my eyes, once affected, could not stand any strain in the evening.

I saw no hope. One monotonous day followed

another. The same dull mornings, hurry to the shop, — the same dangerously crowded cars, the same people in the shop, — the same machine, everything the same day after day. Oh, how sickening, how hateful!

My brother also became nervous. He was much discouraged from walking around in the streets day in, day out, looking for work. When at last he found one job he left it in two days. I remember in what angry excitement I found him when I returned from work.

"What happened?" I asked.

"I left my position. The boss wanted me to make a bum job and I refused. This morning when I was sent to fix a pipe in a cellar, the boss told me to be ready with it in half an hour. When I was on the job I found that the alteration needed at least an hour's time or else the pipe would burst again in a few days. The woman complained to me that she had had the pipe fixed two or three times during the last month and that it burst again soon after it was fixed. I promised her to make a good job. While I was working, the boss came in.

"'What is it you are doing in here so long?' he asked me.

"'This pipe needs to be cleaned thoroughly before we put the zinc in, or it'll burst,' I answered.

"'Fool that you are! You don't mean to fix the pipe so it should keep for a year, do you? If you make such jobs everywhere, the pipes would never break. Do you expect to make business that way? Fine business man! Come on, finish it up.'

"I protested. 'Mr. Boss,' I said, 'you are paid to make a good job, not to spoil it.'

"'None of your business what I'm paid for; do as I tell you or go where you came from!'

"So I went where I came from. Would you expect me to do otherwise?"

I was silent for a moment, thinking what to answer him. Was he right or wrong? Surely he was right, but where could he find a boss who does not do "business"?

"You know, Sam," I said, "you are not working for almost six months. You must at last find a job —"

He did not let me finish.

"You, whom I always thought the most ideal girl, should speak that way!"

"No, I mean that you must do it until you are able to stand on your own feet, and do as you like — that is, until you are able to work for yourself, not for the boss!"

He misunderstood me.

"I know what you mean. You are tired of giving me the four dollars a week. I don't need them! I don't need them! Never again will I take your money, you can keep it for yourself!" he cried out in anger and left the room.

It was the second time since he came that we had

quarrelled. I did not mean to hurt him. He misunderstood me when I only wanted to advise him. But was not I a little too hard to him? The poor boy thought I was tired of him. How would I feel in his position? Tears of regret began to flow from my eyes. Oh, miserable, miserable life, when will all that end! For a whole week my brother did not speak to me, neither did he accept my money. At last, through the aid of a girl friend who worked in the same shop with me, I made him come back to me. After a long talk with him I decided to send him away to Toronto, Canada, where my eldest brother had recently arrived from Russia. I thought that perhaps there near my brother he might be able to find a job. The problem was how to send him. The immigration office in Canada was very careful not to admit people without money. A friend of mine from Toronto happened to visit New York at that time and he took my brother along with him on his way back.

I can never forget the expression in his eyes when he bade his last good-bye to me. They were full of love and gratitude to me, full of fear for the new country he was going to enter, not knowing what the change would bring him. That helpless, lonely look in his eyes was heart-breaking, that fear to enter another strange country among unknown people. I was the only comfort he had had since he left home, and even me he was losing now.

"Cheer up, boy, you are going to begin a new life. I'm so sure that in a short time we'll meet again, and I'll see you happy and contented," I tried to comfort him.

He was silent, his eyes watched me all the time. He entered the train like one who enters a place of sure death. A deep sigh drew out of his breast when the train moved. That sigh cried to me, "Oh, where will I be thrown now?"

Downcast and broken-hearted, I returned home. "Was it right to let him go away from me? He is so young and inexperienced in life, what will happen to him there?" I thought. My elder brother was a man of a cool character — quite a contrast to the rest of our family. Besides, he was a married man and had to mind his own family, and being himself a newcomer, I was afraid that he would not be able to take care of my younger brother, and it worried me very much. But what could I do? I was glad to give him my last cent, but that did not help him. It was suicidal to him to walk around for days and days without work. Perhaps there in Toronto where the unemployment is not so horrible, he would at last get something to do. Trying to comfort myself with that hope, I fell asleep. The next morning I awoke with my usual headache. I could hardly raise my head, and wanted to stay home, but as it was Saturday and we only worked till one o'clock, I went to work.

A girl friend asked me to accompany her to the opera. She had never heard Caruso, and now, as she was going to leave for Switzerland the next month to be married there, she wanted to hear him before her departure. I willingly accepted her invitation. We went to the opera and stood in the crowded line for general admission. It happened to rain hard and while I was protected with an umbrella, my feet were soaked through my open soles. But what did it matter? Caruso and the best star cast were singing. What more did I want? — Hundreds of us stood behind the orchestra around the rails enjoying the music on foot. Here were crowds of all kinds of toilers, who after a day's hard work came to stand on their feet for another few hours to sweeten their sorrow with music.

At the end of the second act I was overtaken with feverish chills. I grew tired and seated myself on a rail near the aisle. An old gentleman passed and bent over to me.

"Are you tired, young lady? Would you like to use my seat? I am leaving now."

I thanked him heartily and went to look for the number marked on the check. It was D, number 20, — a very comfortable chair near to the stage. But no sooner had I sat down than two middle-aged ladies frowned at me through their lorgnettes and called for the usher. The usher immediately responded, and noticing me he asked in surprise: —

"Why — your ticket, ma'm?"

I showed him the ticket.

"I'm sorry, but you can't have this seat," he said, after examining my ticket.

"Why can't I? This ticket entitles me to it," I replied indignantly. 'It was given to me and I have a right to it."

"But you can't sit here," he argued; "these ladies object to your sitting here because you are not dressed decently."

"But I did not come here to exhibit my clothes. I came to hear the opera," I said angrily.

But he would not let me stay, and to avoid a scene I dragged my tired legs back to the standing place. I looked at my dress, then I looked up and around at the "decency" — in the orchestra and boxes — and I understood. My arms and shoulders were not exposed — that's why I was not dressed decently.

I could no more listen to the music. I was nervous and embittered. Can any one convince me that they had a right to object to me, when I had the ticket? Can I ever forgive that aristocratic "decency" which deprived me of the chair that was so gently offered to me when I was tired out, hardly having strength enough to stand on my water-soaked feet?

Those high-class ladies who never earned the silk and gold laces they had on, who were kept by their parents or by their husbands, who would be lost if they were not supported, objected to me that worked so hard for even the shabby dress that I had on.

My heart was bubbling with anger and feeling of injustice. Why had I not a right to the music that I liked so much? They deprived me of my little recreation that I so seldom got. And while I stood leaning on the rail, I was seized with a new ambition — an ambition to get rich and buy up a number of seats among the richest, and place on those chairs people with shabby clothes. And to show that "shabbiness" perhaps understands and feels music more than "gold embroidered chiffons."

The next day I was in bed enjoying a fine cold. I could allow myself that luxury, for it was Sunday. I did not know I had the grippe, and on Monday I went to work. I thought it was only a plain cold, and for such I could not afford to stay home in the height of the season. It was the last days in March. There was one more busy month to end the spring season, then — slack season again. If I had worked regularly as the others did, I would perhaps have had a few dollars saved up, but now what am I to do, what am I to do, when the dull season will approach me? With the last bit of my strength I rushed my work, trying to make up for loss of time.

As if the vision of "slack" had the same meaning for everybody, so the girls were rushing more than ever. Bundles were flying from hand to hand, waists were slipping from the machines into the baskets, from the baskets to the counter. The girls were bent low over their machines, as if nothing else mattered to them; their talking ceased, only their singing encouragingly speeded the ponderous machines as if driving them quicker. The forelady ran from one table to the other as if in a frenzy — all was rush — and we were in it.

But all that humdrum rush, the buzzing noise, suddenly stopped. I came in to work one morning and found the girls in a peculiarly excited condition. Each looked at the other so strangely. The girls on my table scarcely worked. Some of them were dressed in black. It was unusually quiet: no laughter, no songs to accompany the noisy machinery. The faces of all were so serious and sad.

"What happened?" I asked my neighbor.

"Why it's the 25th of March to-day!"

"The 25th of March — so what is that?"

She looked at me unpleasantly surprised. I felt very weak that morning and was indifferent to questioning any more. I absorbed myself in the work and I could hardly notice what was going on around me.

Suddenly my neighbor pulled my sleeve. "Why don't you stand up?"

I raised my head. All the people in the shop stood on their feet, mournfully looking at each other. Instinctively I jumped up. We stood that way for a few seconds. Tears were in the people's eyes when they went back to work. I felt ashamed to ask my neighbor again. From the way she looked at me I understood that any waist-maker should know what the 25th of March was. As I sat puzzled, the word "Triangle" was pronounced somewhere behind me. I thrilled with terror! It struck me immediately — the memorial day of the hundred and forty-seven young workers who lost their lives on the 25th of March in the year 1911. How stupid was I not to guess it at once in the morning when I entered the shop!

When that catastrophe occurred I was home in Russia. I still remember what a panic that news caused in our town when it first came. Many a family had their young daughters in all parts of the United States who worked in shops. And as the most of those old parents had an idea of America as one big town,[1] each of them was almost sure that their daughter was a victim of that terrible catastrophe. Their tears never dried until they at last received letters from their children that they were alive. So it was the 25th of March

[1] I remember when I left my home for Canada an old woman neighbor of ours came over with a sponge cake, asking me the favor to take the cake along with me and deliver it to her girl, who lived in New York. I told her I was not going to New York, but to Canada. "Oh, it's all right, my child, America is one world! You'll find her, you'll surely recognize her."

to-day! In the same day three years ago one hundred and forty-seven girls were burned alive! I could work no more. My machine, the work, the shop, and the people all faded, and before me stood out the picture of Waverly Place where the big Ash Building was embraced in fire tongues. Hundreds of people crowded the windows crying piteously for help. The doors were locked, no fire escapes in all the building. Most of the men were quick enough to get into the elevators and were saved. Those girls who could not push themselves through to the elevators jumped through the windows and were killed. The rest were burned.

Impatiently I waited for that evening. I wanted to know more about the Triangle. I wanted to know what kind of a shop it was before and after the fire. I knew that our union had a memorial meeting for the hundred and forty-seven innocent victims that evening and was anxious to be present and know more about it. After six o'clock I went to the union office and entered the manager's room. He had his hat and coat on ready to leave. "No complaints to-night, little friend! I must hurry to the meeting," he said.

"Oh, please, just for a few minutes. You are dealing with the Triangle since 1913. You know all about that firm in the past. Will you not tell me about it. I want so much to know of the conditions prevailing there now and before."

I spoke with such urgency that he could not refuse. "Come on for supper with me if you wish. We'll talk while eating," he said.

I gladly consented. In the restaurant in a far corner, at a small table, there we sat silent for a long while until he at last began, his deep, expressive eyes sadly gazing into space while he spoke: —

"For years and years our union had a hard fight with the Triangle Waist Company. The most miserable conditions that could be imagined prevailed in the Triangle shops. [Directly the bosses had very little to do with the workers. They kept men inside contractors. Each man had a set of ten or twelve girls, who worked under him. Those men were the actual employees of the Triangle. The people worked the longest hours, getting two and three dollars a week. The discipline there was of the severest. The doors were locked from soon after eight in the morning till lunch hour. If any girl happened to be a few minutes late after lunch, the door was locked against her till the next morning. No one was allowed to leave the shop during working hours.]

"The sub-contractors always tried to get in newly arrived immigrants — people without any knowledge of the English language and American life — people who were helpless and lived at the mercy of the bosses, who only gave them enough to keep soul and body together. Their time and freedom belonged to the boss. Like locked-up prisoners they sat working in the shop — a place without the slightest protection for their lives. And when at last the people could not stand any longer such slavery, they went down on strike, demanding a little of their human rights. For twenty weeks the firm fought them bitterly, trying to break the strike. They hired gangsters to make riots and fight the pickets, and when the men gangsters would be afraid to beat girls, the firm went so far as to hire immoral women to beat the pickets. The union, at this time being very small and weak, tried her best to help the strikers. For the first time the union called a general strike, and though many shops were organized, the Triangle remained as it was. The strike was broken, the people returned to work on the previous conditions. Again the people worked for three dollars a week. Again they slaved behind locked doors. The cuttings of the goods were always heaped up around the tables. The smallest spark could inflame all the building in a minute. The people never thought of it. Their struggle for mere existence could not make them realize in what danger they were every minute of the day in case of fire. While in the union shops the people worked on Saturday till one o'clock in the afternoon, in the non-union shops, including the Triangle, the people worked till five. The fire broke out on Saturday between three and four in the afternoon, and before the people had time to get up from their machines the house was all in flames. The foremen and contractors, who had the keys of the doors with them, forgot to think of the people. They hastened to save their own lives, leaving the people to the mercy of the fire. And oh, —"

Here he stopped for a while, his teeth gnashing, his eyes sparkling fire.

"Who only saw that panic could never forget it. The heart-breaking cries of the burning girls! It still rings in my ears. Like wounded animals they ran from one door to another, knocking, calling for help, but all in vain.

"Down the street, around the building, thousands of people stood, but could not help. Women fainted and cried in the streets. The unfortunate parents of the victims ran around in a frenzy.

"Suddenly — a terrible cry — 'My child! Oh, my child!' a mother stood near me clasping her hands in agony, and looking wildly up at the burning building where her daughter stood near the window, her hands outstretched.

"'Mother, mother!' she cried, and jumped out through the window. One instant — and she lay crushed to death on the sidewalk. Her mother, falling on the body, was immediately stricken with insanity. A few seconds later four girls clasped their arms and jumped. Their heads were crushed, their arms still clasped around each other. The rest of the girls, seeing their co-workers killed on the sidewalk, were afraid to jump, and they found their death in fire."

He stopped. Tears were in his eyes. He did not touch his supper. Neither did I.

"To think that the Triangle bosses were so heartless, when only on Saturday that terrible catastrophe occurred; when all the city mourned; when the burned and mutilated bodies still lay on the street, — those bosses were so shameless as to come out with an advertisement the following Monday, notifying the people that they were ready for business in their new office! Ready for business again, so soon after the horrible death of a hundred and forty-seven young beings! They could have foreseen the danger in not having fire-escapes, in not cleaning up the heaped-up scraps of goods. They did not care. They kept the doors closed so that a worker should not be able to leave during working hours — and soon after that fire the Triangle opened that shop again. The factory's contractors got other newly arrived innocent young immigrants. They made these girls work the same long hours, for the same starvation wages, under the same strong discipline as before.

"Memorial meetings were held all over. Social workers and other sympathizers were present at these meetings. They condemned the Triangle and many other factories where the workers were in danger, every minute in the day, of being fried on the capitalistic frying-pan. They promised to do all in their power to help the workers to protect their lives. But soon after the bodies were buried, and the memorial meetings were over, everything quieted.

"At present, when the Board of Sanitary Control is in existence, the sanitary conditions are considerably improved, but only a small number of the factories are absolutely safe from fire. Most of them are still dangerous."

For a long while he was silent, his eyes still fixed in the distance.

"How is the Triangle at present?" I broke the silence.

"Oh," he began, "in 1913 the Triangle joined the Manufacturers' Association, and had the people in that factory been fully organized, they would have benefited from the protocol as the organized workers did. It was strongly believed that after such wholesale slaughter as had occurred, the people would at last awake, they would at last open wide their eyes and see what life they live in, see who and what is depriving them of their happiness and liberty, stand up and, with their joint power, free themselves from the legal criminals and create a better world, and lead a better life; but unfortunately they do not yet realize, — they still lack self-consciousness. They still have the slaving spirit of their fathers and forefathers — the spirit that calls only for obedience. They are afraid to organize, because the non-union people are more favored.

"Though the Triangle Waist Company is a protocol shop, it is still one of the worst shops in the waist and dress industry. The people are still week workers, working on the section system under the control of inside contractors. We have tried our best to abolish the inside contracting system, but it is very hard to accomplish. This firm is practicing the contracting secretly, and is careful enough not to have the contractors on the business record as contractors, but as ordinary individual employees. If we receive a complaint from a girl in the shop that she works for a contractor and we take the matter up, we seldom succeed with it. I, together with the chief clerk of the Manufacturers' Association, was up a few times in that shop to find out about it. The firm would always deny the charge. On the record the contractors are entered as plain operators, and though we know they are contractors, we are not able to fight, for it is impossible to establish the real facts."

It was very late when we left the restaurant, but I did not go home. Carelessly we wandered along the sound-asleep dark streets, each one absorbed in heavy thoughts. I felt downhearted, and a hopeless mood spread over me.

I felt pained for the hundred and forty-seven

dead victims, and still more for the millions of live victims of the present capitalistic system. Who, after all, is responsible for such murders? Where is the law to prosecute the murderers — Triangle bosses? Who is to remove those black wings which spread over the lives of the young, hopeful men who lost their brides, their future wives in that fire? Who is to remove those wings of misfortune that spread over the homes of the unfortunate fathers and mothers who lost their children, — their pride, — their bread-winners? From the Russian autocratic weapons those parents ran to save their children; from hunger, from disease they saved their little ones — to "free America" they fled; only to bring their children to the altar of capitalism! In front of their eyes their children were burning! Over a hundred future mothers of American citizens were murdered! But that was not the only disaster.

Many thousands of American citizens who struck in Lawrence and in Paterson and in Colorado for a better life were cruelly beaten, and some killed.

Where was the Government to protect its citizens? Why is the Government so indifferent to the miserable lives of those who produce the enormous wealth of the country? Is this a country free only for capitalists who have the real power? We are not citizens, but free slaves! In times of slavery, the people belonged to the master directly.

Whose are we now? Don't we belong to the master indirectly? We come and beg, we offer our hands, our brains, our energy, and our freedom for sale. In times of slavery the master would sell his people if he pleased; now the people are compelled to sell themselves!

CHAPTER XVII

MY cold became worse at the end of the week, and on Saturday morning I lay in bed burning with fever. I grew hot; I felt thirsty and hungry, and I could not move. Not a soul around me — no one knew I was sick. The loneliness choked me. In my feverish agony I imagined that no one cared about me. I felt alone and deserted. Oh! how I longed for a warm, motherly hand, for a warm, soothing word in that small, stuffy room, that seemed to grow still smaller in my feverish mind. The walls came close together, and tightened around me, clenching my head. It grew noisy in my ears — in my head — I fell into drowsiness.

Only late the next day the mistress of the house happened to open my door, and found me sick. She brought a doctor, and he ordered me to stay in bed for a week. I had the grippe in a severe form.

I looked like a shadow when I went back to work the second week. I needed a good long rest in order to regain my strength, for I had worked too hard and worried too much for many, many months. But I did not dare to think of it. I was anxious to work and pay up the rest of my debt. It lay upon my mind as a heavy burden, and I had to get rid of it. I made the biggest pay in my entire career as waist-maker the second week in April — eighteen dollars! Then the next week it turned slow all of a sudden.

Another first of May approached. In my present shop I did not have to agitate the girls to stop from work and keep holiday. They were quite enthusiastic about the first of May themselves, and made great preparations for the coming holiday. They made up white waists with red collars — a uniform for the parade, all one style, as an expression of solidarity.

Thousands of workers — men, women — joined in the grand march. All held signs of protest against this capitalistic system. There were signs with protest against the brutality of the Rockefeller officers toward the miner-strikers in Colorado. There were also many signs with strong protests against the war that seemed imminent between the United States and Mexico. The people did not want war — they had nothing against the poor Mexicans, who were just as helpless against their bandit capitalists as the people here are helpless. The war would mean more mines, more wealth for the Wall Street magnates, and more widows applying to charity institutions, more orphans coming into the orphan asylums, more insane mothers in the insane asylums — the result of war to the unprotected working-class.

My shop was a new branch of one of the largest firms in the industry — one of the most famous for its sweat conditions. In the busy season we saw none of the actual bosses, except the one who was always in the shop — he was one of the minor partners. Now, when it turned slow, they began to visit our shop very frequently and meddle in everything. Their other shops were similar to the famous Triangle Company, and so they were shocked to find that some girls in our place earned as high as eighteen and twenty dollars a week. To equalize our shop with their others, they began to cut down the prices and enforce new rules. But our girls refused to submit to new rules that would violate the union agreement. Our boss who managed the shop always treated us quite fairly, but now he tried to carry out the instructions of the higher authorities, and disputes between him and the workers began to arise.

I interfered very little in the shop occurrences at that time, for since I had the grippe my health had become worse and worse, and that created in me an awful indifference to everything. I felt too tired to work, too tired to think, too tired to live.

My few friends were very anxious about me. They all advised me to leave town for the country for a few weeks, but I could not take anybody's advice because I had not any money.

My day's existence wholly depended on my day's

work, and tired out though I was, I could not stop. But the second week in May work practically ceased in our shop. We would sit in the shop all day waiting for some work that came in from time to time, giving us occupation for one or two hours. While waiting, the girls busied themselves in making their own clothes. They would buy up all the remnants left in the shop, or hunt up bargains in the various department-store basements, and prepare their own summer outfits.

It made one wonder to watch with what endeavor they tried to piece out waists of the smallest remnants, copying the styles from our shop. Seldom could a girl (unless she was a "swell") afford to buy a waist in our shop, for though we made them, they were too expensive for us, and we had to find satisfaction in cheaper imitations. In one of these basement bargains, some of my shopmates fitted me into a dress made of various pieces of cotton voile; the cost of it all amounted to sixty cents, and while they fitted it on me, they teased me, saying, "Now you are ready for the country — upon our words, with this dress on, you'll have all them fellows out there after you."

Those magic words — country, vacation, fellows — were occasionally mentioned while the girls were helping each other with the fitting. They spoke with great relish of the good times of last year, telling one another of their experiences in the country.

"Say, you was in the Y.W.'s country place last summer, — is it good?" some one asked her neighbor.

"Good for nothin'," her neighbor answered. "Never again to them 'charity pleasures'! I get enough living in the Association all the year around. You ain't got a thimble's full o' freedom. There is rules for everything — sleep, eat, wake up — all rules. We get to think that we are nothin' but rules. We only get two weeks' vacation in all them twelve months, and we like to enjoy it, and forget everything, but there you can't. They make you work cause you only pay three dollars a week, and jus' when you are outside runnin' around, havin' a good time, they call you in to set the table, take off the table, or do some other little t'ings. You can't enjoy much, — though you don't work hard, — it's a sort o' duty you don't like to have, when you wan'na be perfectly free. Them charity institutions t'ink they do you a lot o' favors, but they don't, 'specially when you work for the rest of the expenses, and it's still — charity favor."

"Why should you live at the Y.W.'s? I would never stay there, even if they kept me for nothing," said one of the girls who stood aside and listened indulgently to her neighbors' talk. "They keep charity homes for poor working-girls. Why don't they see that the working-girl gets paid properly for the work she is doing, and need not live in a charity home? Our rich employers give charity by underpaying us; for our money they get fame and praise — eh, if they only paid us what we deserved, we could get comfortable homes without their help; with our money they are kind and charitable."

"You are perfectly right," the inmate of the Y.W.C.A. assented, and as if unwilling to be switched off the main subject she turned to her first questioner: "You been in Connedicut for your vacation; how did you like it?"

"Nothin' doin' in Connecticut for me this summer. I'm goin' to the mountains. It's been a rotten boarding-place. Mind you, not even a decent dancin' hall, and only two 'n' half fellows to a dosend girls. There ain't much fun in dancin' with girls," she remarked.

"That's right, dem cheap countries is good for nothing," another girl remarked with authority. "You come with me, where I was last summer. My! they got some dancin' hall, and fresh eggs and chicken every day, and lots of fellows too. We'd hardly skip a night — we'd dance till twelve and one at night," she finished with relish.

"Where is that country of yours?" a few girls asked her anxiously.

"Why, it's right in the Catskill Mountains in Sullivan County."

I had time enough to observe and listen to their talks and found that only a few of us were there to whom country meant a nice, quiet resting-place, where one could leisurely breathe the fresh air. To the great many girls who are deprived all the year around of proper recreation, the country is like a big, exciting reception for which they are preparing themselves for weeks ahead — country to them meant fresh-laid eggs for breakfast, chicken for dinner, and a dancing hall to dance away their vacation —

And such was their life — such was the breadth of our world, realized by only a few of us who looked at the others rather indulgently, if not with pity. Still, in their ignorance they were at least happier than we, happier because of their ignorant indifference to their wretched life.

Our days in the shop became more and more monotonous, as we sat waiting for work most of the time. We grew weary of our idleness and of the warm weather, and at last the forelady laid us off for one week. I stopped working altogether. I gave up my room, and, by invitation, went to stay with my friend Alice at her small apartment that I liked so much. She was going to leave the city soon, and wished to have me with her for a while. My friend Alice was a great optimist and tried her best to revive my spirits in me, but I confess it was the hardest task she ever undertook.

My present pessimistic state of mind developed not only from my own sufferings, but also from the life around me. The general conditions of the people among whom I lived filled my heart with misery. My head was always puzzled with the question of inequality in this universe. I was unable to decide what remedy would be best to equalize the world. One thing I understood: that the present capitalistic system must be changed, that the wealth created by people should be divided among those people. But whether the change should come through peaceful education or revolution, I felt not ripe enough to decide.

In the warm spring nights, we would, both sitting on the floor, discuss the social questions. I suffered from sleeplessness the last few weeks, and Alice would often sit up with me all through the night and talk to me. Again she raised the question of my taking up a course in a training school for organizers. The Women's Trade-Union League in Chicago was about to open a school for organizers, and she tried to persuade me to go to Chicago to take up that course. But my enthusiasm for trade-unionism had somewhat diminished lately. As my friend Fannie once felt, so I now began to feel, that its progress was very slow. Besides, my health failed me, and that made it almost impossible for me to study while I had to support myself meantime.

One Sunday evening my friend Alice asked me if I would not like to hear Mother Jones, who had recently returned from Colorado where the big miners' strike was going on. I had heard about Mother Jones so much. Mother Jones — the Angel of the Miners, as she was called — is a woman of eighty-two years of age. All her life long, she goes from one State to the other where the coal industry prevails, bringing light and courage to the unfortunate coal miners who are made industrial serfs by the mine magnates.

We went to that meeting. The hall was overcrowded. In my mind I pictured the eighty-two-years-old "Mother" as a tall, big, strong woman.

I stood, waiting impatiently. "Mother Jones" the chairman announced — and in walked an old, old, bent lady, accompanied by two men on whose arms she leaned. A deeply wrinkled face, a few white hairs left on her head — she showed her eighty-two years. Slowly she walked over to the platform.

It was very warm, the air was thick, which made her breathing heavy. In a trembling, hardly audible voice she began to talk. We were all very silent, trying to catch the words; but as she went deeper into her subject her voice rose louder and louder, the words came out clearer, the expression forcible. The eighty-two-years-old lady had slowly vanished. Before me stood a woman full of embitterment against the powers which allowed her children in West Virginia to be treated so brutally years before, and in Colorado now — a woman filled with revenge against those who tortured her "sons." Before me stood an agitator with enormous power; a labor leader who carried the bright future of the working-class. She hypnotized us. She carried us with her to the fields of Colorado. Here we saw the miners working in the dark, dangerous caverns, where they risk their lives every minute in the day, — here are the miners out on strike demanding human conditions, — here are the sheriffs and other guards who kill the strikers, drive them out of the homes, destroy their property, — here are a number of tents where the wives and children of the strikers were sheltered, only to be burned in the fire following the conflict between the state militia and the strikers.

"Me — a weak woman of eighty-two years — they locked up in a cell, so that I should not be able to stand and fight with my boys!" (She calls all the miners her boys.) "For days and days they kept me in that dark, damp cell; for nine long days I had to fight with the hungry rats! They thought that a woman eighty-two years old would be too weak to overcome it. They intended to weaken me that way! But in those nine long days of starvation, in those nine long days and sleepless nights, I grew stronger; with more hate against the high-class burglars, with more readiness to stand with my boys and fight, fight to the last!

"Afterwards, when they released me, they ordered me out of the State. I protested, for who has a right to send me out of a place where I lived for eighty-two years? Of all the citizens I was the oldest! But again I was locked up for eleven days, again they starved me, and after those eleven days, they put me on a train and sent me out of the State!"

As she spoke, I forgot that I was hearing all that of "free America"! I found myself in Russia where exactly the same brutality is practised! Dark, autocratic Russia — and light, free America! There the people are persecuted for free speech, they are exiled to Siberia. What is here? Is it not the same, only in a different form?

How I admired that little, old woman with so much youthful spirit in her! How I admired her courage! A woman of eighty-two years, and so active — so full of energy! She seemed to have put new courage into me. I felt more hopeful. She was eighty-two, — I was twenty-one; — there was time for me. I said to my friend Alice that night, as we both lay sleepless, "I am going to try my strength and ability."

"Hurrah!" she exclaimed, and we shook hands.

The next day we sat making our plans. We both agreed that I must grow strong physically before I began to do anything. We decided that I should go to the country for a month and go to Chicago afterwards. There I hoped to find work and attend the school of the Women's Trade-Union League. For that purpose Alice gave me fifty dollars. In a few days we parted. She went back to Canada, and I began to look for a reasonable country place.

It happened that a married sister of mine was to come over from Russia to join her husband who lived in Newark. I delayed my trip, waiting for her to come. I looked forward to our meeting, thrilling with a desire to see her, to hear some of the news from home, — that dear spot from which I had been torn away for more than two years, — to recall together with her, the sweet recollections of my early unhappy yet happy life: my home that I missed so much in the gray, monotonous, slack days, when I paced the city from one end to the other, searching vainly for work. In those days, when tired, exhausted, half-starved, I would return home, facing four narrow, lonely walls. In those days, when I lay sick, burning with fever, lonely and forsaken, — oh! how I craved for my home, to feel on my burning head my mother's soft hand as a healing compress — my father's gentle smile as a balsam to my wounded heart.

I close my eyes, and I see my father — the mild, peaceful expression in his deep, gray eyes, a divine smile resting on his lips — hard life seemed insignificant to him.

My mother — her tired, nervous, always anxious,

often frowning, face, a pair of sorrowful black eyes, sadly carrying the brunt of life. Of both their lives, hers was the harder. From the time of her marriage she hardly had a care-free day — bearing children every two years, she fought with the measles, scarlet fever, typhoid fever, coughs and various other colds; she fed them, she clothed them. She gave life to thirteen children, of whom she buried four. Knowledge, wisdom, for her children she placed highest. I remember with what particular sweetness she bent over a sleepless child. She would always sing the same famous old Jewish cradle-song that so well symbolizes the love of the Jews for knowledge and wisdom: —

> "A little, white goat stood under your cradle,
> With raisins and nuts the goat went to peddle; —
> But you, my child, will study wisdom,
> For knowledge is of all business best,
> A pious, honest, and learned Jew —
> You shall forever last." [1]

She never saw a bright day until her children grew up. And then — Her oldest boy was in the hated Russian army, another was in prison for carrying the message of Freedom, three children scattered in far-away America — this was the reward of her long years of struggle and hope for happiness, that might have come through her children. She waited patiently. She had strong faith in her God. She believed in the Almighty. She prayed,

[1] Translated from the Yiddish.

prayed all her life to him. And each new-coming blow she took as the will of God. "So does God want — such is His wish. God will help — God is pitying."

But as the long years wore on, and life became harder with no relief, a thought of suspicion would often secretly creep into that pure heart. And the tired-out God's martyr would repine and curse the day that brought her into life.

I remember when my father was once boycotted (he was boycotted twice in his life on account of his liberal views on religion and education), he left town to start a school somewhere else. My mother was left penniless with seven children. Our house caught fire one night, and was destroyed, all except two rooms that served as a refuge until father was brought back and we were able to rebuild it.

Though only five years old at that time, I clearly remember how one late autumn night, a thunderstorm broke out. Five of us children were sitting on a sofa near the brick oven, hungry, shivering with fright and cold. Mother and the two oldest children were out.

The rain poured down, soaking the ceiling. Pieces of plaster kept falling on us and on the beds. Mother entered, her shawl dripping with water. She gave a glance at the ceiling and at us smeared with plaster, and she clasped her hands in agony at the disaster.

Raising her eyes she cried out, "O Almighty, if you can't make an end to this, make an end to my life; take me away with all of them — my innocent birds."

It was wonderful how father, through such long years of hardship, kept up his serenity. He must have had iron nerves. I seldom remember him without his peaceful smile, that smile that made his pupils adore him. He was a born teacher.

In those days the Hebrew schools were kept open from eight in the morning till eight in the evening. Children from the age of seven were kept in school for such long hours, and made to study hard. Bright children of nine and ten were taught the Talmud. It was absolutely reckless for such young, delicate brains to deal with the seriousness of the Talmud, and my father opposed the custom, but with no success. There was no break in the studies except for their dinner. I remember those poor young creatures — those thin, pale-faced, tired scholars of such a tender age. My father had long realized that such a system was ruinous to the health of the children. He tried to induce the other schoolmasters to introduce games and songs and cited for argument the blooming health of the children in the Russian public schools. But he was only laughed at.

The orthodox Jews of our town at that time declared him a sinner. Jewish children were to be taught the Torah, but no games, no songs. My father, however, began to introduce games into his own school. I remember with what impatient, gleaming eyes those little animals awaited the play-hour. When in the afternoon their big, old "rabi" would leave his "cathedra," they all surrounded him and played and sang together. But their happiness soon ended.

One morning leaflets were hung up in the synagogue announcing that father was leading the children to sin — that instead of teaching the Torah, he is spending his time in play. And my father was boycotted. But a year later the town realized that his methods were essential. They realized what effect the play had on the children, and they sent for him. They brought him back with honor — and, bless his heart, he is still engaged in teaching and playing with his pupils — mostly beginners.

He still spends his evenings in thinking of newer reforms for the Hebrew beginners' school. He is an artist in dealing with beginners, and they adore him. He is even known among the very small children who never saw him. A mother in our town could rule the most mischievous child by warning him that he would not be sent to my father's school unless he behaved.

The meeting with my sister was far from being happy. She did not expect to find me so thin and worn out. She felt hurt and disappointed. I tried to be cheerful and happy.

"Now, you are going to stay with me, and let me look after you; for I promised mother to keep you with us. She wants us all to be together, and take care of one another," she begged me. "Mother has grown very old since you left; also father has turned gray. They could not get accustomed to it for a long, long time. You were the first one to make the break, and little by little four of us have strayed away from home. Israel is in the army — and at that once long, overcrowded table, only four small children are left.

"All week long father and mother are busy — but the Sabbath meal — oh, that is a very miserable hour for mother. She misses us greatly. The empty chairs make the room so gloomy, and mother never ceases to cry. She always places your photograph near her at the table."

Oh, my mother, if I were only able to repay you for your noble sacrifices, for all the injustice we did to you by running away to look for our own happiness. You saint soul! I would give my life to make you happy, to make your hopes, your dreams come true. But mother's happiness is her children's happiness. What must I do to be happy for her sake? What must I do to outgrow misery?

To stay with my sister, I had to play the game of contentment, and that I could not very often do.

For my mother's sake, I had to hide from her my financial nakedness; and to make her believe that nothing was wrong with me, I bought her a present for ten dollars, never telling her that they were borrowed.

CHAPTER XVIII

A WEEK later I was off to a farm near Princeton, the farmer's family being my country people.

For the first time since I left my home, I saw the country again. With bewildered, hungry eyes, I stood there the first morning, looking around me. My heart thrilled with joy, when, after so many, many months of sickening city life, I again faced those spacious green fields.

The sun was widely spread over the horizon; hundreds of birds were singing and twittering their morning songs, flying from one place to another; tiny little chicks ran around in the yard, digging their beaks into the soft ground, searching for worms. There were cherry trees loaded with ripe white cherries. The grass spread a fresh, dewy fragrance, and everything around was full of life, fresh life, real life!

I did not know what to do. I began to jump around singing and whistling in accord with the birds. I felt happy. I forgot that only yesterday I came from the city. It seemed as if I was born here, and grew up among these trees, these spacious fields, these clear skies.

After breakfast I and a few other girls, who were

also spending their vacation here, went to the near-by canal, that cut through the woods. Deep in the shade of magnificent old oaks, majestically spreading their branches over the water, where the restful shade mingled with the golden sunrays; there the canal was hidden, protected on the other side by a young, leafy grove.

Glowing days, wonderful days followed! We had a rowboat, fishing-lines — all we wanted for our enjoyment. Away from civilization, from artificiality, we ran around all day in our loose bathing-suits, singing merrily, jumping around like wild goats. We were free, we belonged to ourselves, and we enjoyed it immensely!

Very often, when I grew tired of running around, I would hide myself in the deep shadows under a tree, and lie there for hours and hours, wrapped in illusions, lulled by the quiet rustling of the grass and gentle zephyr winds in the trees. The leaves would sway and bend to each other as if for a kiss, — the grass would flutter and its sweet murmurs would fill my heart with deep, mysterious feelings. I understood its whispers — it murmured of Nature's might, of its constant activity, of the summer to go, and summer to come — of eternal life — of love — happy romance —

From time to time a busy bee passed, buzzing around, or a bird singing, its flute-like voice melting into quaverings, would stop to rest on a branch.

How wonderful it was to lie there, lulled by those sweet sounds, embraced by nature, and dream — dream of happiness and love —

Yes, love — Who, at twenty-one, — when from the youthful blossom the woman is rapidly awakening, when the heart is bubbling over with emotions, the soul wrapped in dreams, — does not secretly crave for a sympathetic some one? For some one who understands and loves? Who at that age does not crave for a mate — to go hand in hand into life's path, to share its burdens, to share its pleasure?

In the city where the burden of existence weighed heavily on me, where day in and day out I lived in the ugly reality of poverty, where before me passed, back and forth, the down-trodden, cursed humanity, I had little thought for love. I was wrapped in misery, ugly misery!

Here, in the quiet, wavy grass, in the peacefulness of open nature, my heart began to long, my heart craved for a mate, to go hand in hand against misfortune, to fight against untruthfulness, to rise together to the heights, away, away from this hateful, toiling world, where the noblest callings are crushed under the exploiting capitalistic hammer, where humanity and love are turned into dollars —

As time passed and my vacation drew near its close, I grew more thoughtful. Another week and I would be back in the noise, back in the dirty, airless dwellings, back to the mish-mash that is called "civilization." Oh, how I hated it, how I hated this present kind of civilization!

The other girls also began to get ready for the city. I had not paid much attention to them until now. Making my own meals for economy's sake, while they boarded, I seldom sat at the same table with them. On the days when there were guests to spend the week-ends, the other girls would dress up in their best, while I climbed a cherry or apple tree, and sitting on a branch, would read undisturbed. They thought it very bad manners; they also thought it was bad manners when I, believing myself the best chaperon, would go off fishing alone with the farmer boys.

Now that I thought more of the city, I became more interested in the girls, for their faces also expressed regret to leave the full freedom of the country that they had so much enjoyed for a short time.

Our conversation began unexpectedly. It was late one night — a wonderful July night when the moon appears in its full charm, illuminating the sleeping world. In such a night of quiet peacefulness, full of mysterious charm, — when the heart beats with thirst for life, for love, for sympathy, — when the soul is deeply sunk in melancholy, and the mind is wholly submitted to the sentimental heart's desires, I lay in my bed sleepless. In vain did I try to fall asleep — that wonderful night lured me to the garden, where the flowers covered with night-dew shed such an intoxicating fragrance. Slipping a gown on, I went out. It was light as midday. The trees of the near-by forests threw gigantic shadows over the fields, making the night more mysterious. A feeling of loneliness crept into my heart. The quietness frightened me. On such a night the lonely heart seeks for another heart to be near — to walk silently together through the field, bathed in moonlight, to walk into the wide farness, and to dream — dream of freedom and love — of perfection, of harmony in this world.

Back and forth over the small garden path I walked, until, tired, I went to the front porch to rest.

There, wrapped in blankets, their eyes wide open, looking wistfully at the moon, the three girls lay silently stretched on the floor. I joined them. They were all affected by the moon's glory. They too were melancholy. For a long time, we were all silent, until, at last, I broke the silence.

"Well, girls, I think it is good-bye soon, is it not?"

"Oh, yes," reluctantly one assented with a deep sigh.

"To think that we got to work like horses all the year round, and prepare and save up money just to have enough for two or three weeks' vacation, and when the vacation at last comes, the time runs so quickly that before you get time to look around, — there! you must go back to work," complained another girl.

Poor creature, she just expressed what many of the girls felt; she was only one of them, one of the many who laboriously bent their heads over the machines, struggling hard, turning their health into scanty earnings, saving from anything and everything, in order to go off to the country for two or three weeks in the summer; and while some of them do it intelligently, — they go to the country for a rest, for all the natural things that the country can give them, — a great many spend weeks of exciting preparations. They deprive themselves of regular meals in order to save enough for a more expensive boarding-house. For weeks ahead they sit up late into the night making dresses, petticoats, and other useless cheap fineries; for they must appear "swell" at those expensive country homes. And, who knows? Fate may bring them together with a decent fellow in an expensive boarding-house; and there are chances of marrying and getting rid of the hated shop and eternal anxiety for a living. So the long, exhausting deprivations, the investment in good clothes, may after all prove profitable.

CHAPTER XIX

MY vacation was to end. What a wonderful change this month of country life had made in me. With hidden joy I saw in the mirror that my face, once more rounded out, had gained its freshness; my eyes again were bright and shiny.

I arrived in New York with stored-up strength and vigor, ready to take life up anew. I had been so wrapt in my own self the past month, so indifferent to everything else, that I had not even cared to read the newspaper, and, of course, was ignorant of the burning news that so suddenly inflamed the world; and, oh! the horror of the news of the European war broke over me like a thunder storm. It was unimaginable! How could it be possible for civilized people of the twentieth century — the children of Christ — to engage in bloodshed; bringing shame and destruction upon humanity; the commandment — "Love thy neighbor" — interpreted with guns, shells, and powder. Why fight, what for? and what will this war bring to me?

And it brought to me — As my mind was swallowed in the whirlpool of those chaotic days, a letter from my parents came to me. Father wrote to me: "Our Hebrew schools are nearly empty, for the fathers who paid for their children's education were taken to war. Your brother is being sent to the front. Nathan, who is such a youth, is being reserved. A fine was imposed on me for Sam, because he failed to appear in answer to the military call. I am not able to pay the fine, so the police have taken away from the house any article they think valuable. We can do nothing but pray to God that He should calm His fury. Mother and I are grateful to God that you and Sam and the others are now in America — in a free, blessed country where there are no tzars and kings to shed people's blood. We don't know what will happen to us next, for every day there is something new to disturb us. We have aged twenty years during this past month, and I fear we shall face starvation before long."

The terror raging at home showered over my head, throwing me into a frenzy. What would become of my family? What will happen to them in the near future? How shall we be able to overcome all that? Oh! heaven and earth, calm thy fury!

My brother taken to war to fight for "his country," to fight for a hated country that deprived nearly seven millions of his brothers of all possible freedom, a country that threw them together into a cursed pale, and tried to deaden and enchain their brains, their most beautiful instincts, their artistic abilities. He was sent to fight for a country that rejected all of his applications ever to enter an educational institution. His highest ambition was to enter a school of fine arts, and he really showed great promise through the little portraits he would paint while still very young. But as a Jew, and, still more, as a penniless one, he never realized his ambition.

When only seventeen years of age, he was once taken prisoner in a midnight assailment, — that was so often practised by the police on peacefully sleeping homes, — and was kept prisoner for three months, then sent out from Odessa as prisoner escorted by gendarmes until he reached home. He was forever forbidden to be seen anywhere except in his home town. But my brother refused to be limited, and the police soon found him either in Kiev or Odessa, and arrest after arrest followed.

And after all this persecution, they sent him to fight and kill — whom? Perhaps another struggling Jew from Germany, a Jew from Austria, from Galicia! He was sent to kill people perhaps of his own race. But who are the others? The German, the Russian, the French, the Austrian, and all the other soldiers? If they are not of his race, they belong to his class — to the class of strugglers who toil and starve in time of peace and whose flesh will now carelessly rot in the muddy trenches.

All my cherished plans for the present had to be given up. I had hoped to go to Chicago, and take up the course in the training school of the Women's Trade-Union League, but anxiety for my people at home compelled me to submit to circumstances. I had to remain in New York and get work immediately, so as to help them out until that madness was over. I felt so sure that the war would not last long. I cherished a blind hope that the people would not stand for it; that they would end the war in three or four months.

The war had upset our industry. The season is usually in full swing in the middle of August, but things seemed very uncertain at that time, and a great many manufacturers were afraid to start. The result was that thousands of girls and men were walking around anxiously searching for work. Upon them, also, fell the burden of war. Their families in the war countries were actually ruined, especially in Poland and Lithuania, where they were driven from their homes by the Russians even before the enemy came. Their properties were destroyed and the people scattered. The poor girls ran around as if in a frenzy from the heart-breaking news, but were unable to help their unfortunate parents.

I returned to my last season's shop with a presentiment that trouble was brewing; which later proved to be true.

It had fallen to my lot to become chairlady for the next season. As I had not interfered in the shop occurrences before, I was not known to my boss, so that my election surprised him. He did not, however, take me very seriously — to quote his own language, I was a "mere slip of a girl," and could easily be managed. In fact, judging from my appearance, every one at first took me for a little girl.

Two weeks passed by very peacefully. The boss said that he liked my method in representing the people, and we settled a great many things agreeably. But when I started to find out what was the matter with the test, that it always came out below the price that the workers demanded, then my troubles began. It very often took us a whole day to bargain with the boss before we could finally come to a satisfactory agreement, and besides prices, there were a great many other things to attend to.

There were nearly two hundred workers divided into different branches as operators, finishers, examiners, ironers, cleaners, lace-cutters, hemstitchers. Each branch had to be carefully looked after. A complaint now came from an ironer who did not receive the scale, now a girl came late and she was sent away, now a girl was discharged for spoiling something unintentionally.

I, as shop representative, had to take up every grievance with the boss. If I failed to settle the matter, I had to report and complain to the union.

All that required a great deal of time, and I was too often distracted from my machine. In the busiest weeks, when the workers were making more money, I was kept busy straightening out difficulties for them. Thus, performing my duty as shop representative, I neglected my duty to myself. The result was that my pay envelope suffered great financial deficit. And here came letters from home, each more distressing than the other. Each word in the letters rose as a cry for help, for support, and it nearly drove me insane. My father's home was assailed frequently. Things that could be of use only to my parents and the children were taken away by the police — a punishment for my brother's failure to appear for military service.

The Government was slowly ruining my parents' home. That humble nest that was created through so many, many years of struggle and hardship in that cursed home of bondage! What was I to do? Neglect the shop? Then we should all suffer. No. I was determined to have order in the shop, to get everything that was coming to the workers according to the agreement, to encourage, to show the workers the value of organization and the strength of unity.

Our General Organization Committee had its hands full that season. A great number of manufacturers broke their agreements with the union. Some of them moved their factories away to

Brooklyn, Newark, Jersey City, and Hoboken. They found there cheap country help, and introduced the section system by which it was easy to train inexperienced workers and pay them the smallest possible wages, leaving the New York organized workers without positions.

Those manufacturers, who only a year and a half ago had pledged themselves, by creating the "Protocol of Peace" and individual agreements, to recognize organized labor, and, together with the union, raise the standards in the industry — those very same people took advantage at the first opportunity to overthrow organized labor, to act in their shops as autocrats, and to ignore the worker's wishes and rights.

We worked very hard to organize those shops. Early in the mornings and in the evenings we — a committee of three and four — would go off to such shops and watch the workers at the entrance, to speak and appeal to them. In a great many places we succeeded; in some we were only laughed at; in others we were arrested for speaking to those unorganized workers.

I remember we once went to Brooklyn to picket a shop at seven in the morning. We found three officers and a half-dozen strangers on the spot. As soon as a worker appeared in sight, before we had time to reach her, some one of those boys would get ahead of us, and triumphantly bring her into the shop under his protection. We were warned by some of them to keep away if we wanted to preserve our heads.

"A black eye or broken head is an easy matter with me, so you better keep away from here," said one, when I approached two girls whom he escorted.

"Listen to me, boy, — I just want to ask you a question: If your mother or sister were working in the shop, and if they were out on strike to better their life, would you fight them for it? Don't you see that we mean no harm? We want to speak to the girls, to explain to them that they took away the positions from over a hundred girls who were on strike in New York."

But he would not listen.

"Hey, what do I care? This is my business; I am paid for it, just as you are paid for your work. I make a living out of it. If you would pay me, I would stand with you. Now, keep away, I say."

"Is it right to make a living this way? To club girls' heads?" I went on stubbornly. But he would not listen to me.

Another boy reached us — he was only a youth with books under his arm. He was a high-school boy, and he, too, made his spending money through breaking strikes, before and after school. He was so young and had such a blooming, handsome face one could hardly believe he already belongs to an underworld gang.

"Listen, young fellow, are you taught this kind of profession in school? I shall follow you to school and ask your principal if he knows what you are doing outside of school," I said to him when he pushed one of the pickets from the sidewalk.

"And I'll cut your short legs before you make an attempt to do it," he replied triumphantly.

"Let her try, and she'll never forget it," said another.

I really wanted to follow that boy to school, but I knew what I'd be apt to get, for those boys usually carry out their threats. I recalled that during the past two weeks some of our girls had been beaten by those hired gangsters, and I had no desire to have my face bruised.

The officers separated us in order to avoid trouble. They treated us rather fairly. One policeman called some of us aside, giving us advice.

"Now, girls, you know I sympathize with you, and know what you are here for, but I can't help it. I, as an officer, must see that order prevails. You just don't stand in one place, but walk back and forth on the sidewalk. Speak to the girls while walking. Don't stop them, and if that gang bothers you, I shall show them where to land."

I was astonished at such talk from an officer. My bitter experiences with policemen in former strikes had made me despise them. They very often worked hand in hand with the strike-breakers hired by the employers. While our strikers would peacefully picket the shop, those guards would often make riots, start fights, and in the riots the policemen would arrest innocent strikers, accusing them of making the riot.

It did happen sometimes that strikers in desperation made a riot, but our union strongly forbade and severely warned them against such action. We were always instructed to picket peacefully; but peaceful as we tried to be, we were driven by the policemen from the sidewalks. When I once refused to leave my post, for I had done nothing against the law, the officer unceremoniously pushed me down.

I stood up again, and argued with him, explaining that I knew what I was allowed to do and what I might not do, but he cut me short.

"Hey! I'm telling you to keep away from here if you don't want to be locked up — you fresh thing!"

"I know you can lock me up for no reason, just as you did a great many of the girls," said I calmly, still keeping my place.

Again he pushed me down, lightly striking me with his club.

I felt just a little pain in my shoulder, but my tears began to flow just the same, because I felt hurt, not physically, but for being clubbed for no reason at all.

"You heartless brute!" I murmured through my tears.

"Run along now, run along, unless you want to be arrested," he said gruffly.

I had no desire to be locked up, for I had my duties in the shop. There were a great number of new styles to be settled, and the workers were waiting for me, so I ran along leaving the policeman victor.

The sympathy shown to us by the three officers in Brooklyn made me forget all the grudges I had against police officers. They allowed us to picket, and did not interfere when we spoke to the girls at the entrance. They also watched the gangsters to see that they did not start a fight.

I had no time to breathe those days. From seven to eight-thirty in the morning I was picketing unorganized shops; from eight-thirty to five, I worked in my shop; at five-thirty I was again picketing shops, and at seven in the evening I was at the union office to report various important matters occurring through the day.

As I once mentioned, the commercial unrest at that time caused a crisis in our industry, and the workers more than the manufacturers suffered by it. Only a very few manufacturers had work for a few weeks. Among them was our firm. The latter soon took advantage of the slack period. They knew that hundreds of workers were eagerly looking for work, and, hoping to get cheap labor, they opened a new shop.

The new shop consisted of over a hundred workers, and we immediately realized what it meant to us. Our work was being shifted to the other shop, and we began to sit idle most of our time, as there was not enough business for two shops. I had no objection to sharing the work with the other girls who needed it as much as any of us, but I feared that they might accept a lower wage, thus becoming our competitors.

I had no doubt that the boss purposely opened that shop to get his work cheaper, or else he would not have gone into extra expenses when there was work enough for one shop only.

Fortunately enough for us, the girls of the other shop proved to be conscious of our employer's scheme. They were a true collection of workers thrown out from various shops for their union activity, and, as such, they were harmless to us. They also selected a chairlady and a price committee, who immediately communicated with us, and we demanded from our boss that the same prices for the same garments should be paid in both shops. We refused to deal separately. Our boss accused me of being the responsible person in the shop — for disturbing their daily routine and causing them trouble. He claimed that we had no right to interfere with the other shop. But my answer to him was that if he opened a shop for the purpose of taking away our work, so as to compel us to accept cheaper prices, we had a full right to protest against such unjust action and prevent him from taking advantage of us.

To prevent our working jointly, my boss tried to bribe the workers in the other shop, offering them a bigger price on certain garments, if they would only not communicate with us, but the workers refused. We demanded the same treatment and system in both shops as long as they belonged to one firm and the same work was done.

Our higher bosses raged at me, thinking that it was only I who was responsible for those demands. But I was the shop representative, and spoke not only for myself. I expressed the wish of all the workers in my shop. Still they treated me worse than the others. They tried to rid themselves of me, thinking that with me out of the way, they would accomplish their task, and at the first opportunity I was fired. But I was taken back the same day, for as soon as I took my hat ready to leave the shop, the rush, the noise of the machines, suddenly stopped. Everything came to a standstill. Over two hundred workers folded their hands, quietly protesting against the firm's action. They refused to resume work until their shop delegate returned — and I was taken back the same day. I met the committee of the other shop every day, and we succeeded in working jointly in spite of the opposition on the part of our boss. He made it harder for us from day to day. Times were very bad for the manufacturers, so they made them still worse for the workers.

CHAPTER XX

AS their efforts for getting cheap labor proved a failure, my bosses decided to close up the new shop. We were now confronted with a new and very serious problem. I knew it would be useless to urge my boss to keep up that new shop when rent was so high, power expensive, and all the work there was could easily be made in one shop. Now those girls who so sympathetically coöperated with us would lose their jobs in the midst of the dull season. I shuddered with fear. I knew what it would mean to them to wander around in search of work when the next season was ten weeks ahead.

Why should they be thrown out, why should they have to suffer? Our duty was to share to the last with them. I held a council for that purpose with a committee from the other shop, and we resolved to suggest to our boss that as soon as he closed up that shop he should allow us to divide the work equally with the girls who had been working there; that is, three days for us and three days for the others, so that while we stayed out, the other girls would use our machines, and there would be no extra expense to the boss. We would so share our work until the slack season was over, when those girls could find other jobs.

To my great delight, the boss consented to our plan, and I immediately called a meeting of both shops to inform them of the good news and make preparations for the change. But, oh, how great was my astonishment, how deeply hurt and disappointed I felt, when the workers of my shop, with only a few exceptions, refused to share the work with the others.

"Friends," I exclaimed in great excitement, "I am shocked, deeply shocked at your refusal. You all know what has been going on this season, due to the outbreak of this war that caused a panic in our trade, but more due to the ignorance of so many workers in our industry who refuse to join our ranks, who do not realize the value of organization for themselves. They are living below human standards; they slave for practically no wages; and moreover, they are competing with us organized workers when we so desperately are trying to better our bitter lot. It is due to them that we have so much trouble in our shop, on which our daily existence depends.

"Our bosses are keeping shops for no ideals, but for business! Their anxiety is concentrated, not on giving employment to workers, but on the amount of profit they can clear from their workers; for one more nickel on a garment we sometimes bargain away a whole morning. That is also due to those unorganized workers in other shops who accept a cheaper price, who work longer hours. I do not want to condemn those workers. I know they often repine of their bitter fate. They also would like decent homes, decent clothes, shorter working hours, and to live like human beings, but they are ignorant, they do not know how to change their hard existence. They blindly hope for miracles to happen and lighten their burden.

"But our miracle is in our unity. In our shop I fought very hard for every bit we were to get. And we averted a lot of trouble because we stood united. I have proved to you that only through unity can we help ourselves, but not unity among workers in only one shop. We must be united with all the workers in all the shops throughout the industry. We must help one another to the last.

"When our boss opened up that new shop, he hoped to get cheap help, and if he only succeeded, he would close up our shop and rid himself of all of us, for it pays him better to keep workers who are afraid to contradict him. But fortunately for us, the girls proved to be sympathetic. They treated us with sisterly interest. We united, and they helped us to fight to preserve our standards. Now, when even the boss permits us to share the work, will you refuse? Have you a right to refuse those who helped you? Will you let those girls go now, in the midst of the slack season? Did not any of you here ever experience a slack season and taste its bitterness? I tell you again and again that it is our duty, our human duty, to share our work until they are able to find other jobs!"

There was a short silence. A dark-eyed young girl stood up asking for permission to talk.

"The chairlady, upon my word, made a very good speech, but we ain't goin' to make a livin' on speeches. We did n't had much work this season, and since that shop opened, we ain't got a stitch o' work. Don't we need to make a livin' too? We did not make much of a livin' this season. There ain't enough work for all of us, and we can't help them. We are sorry for the girls, but it ain't our fault that the boss opened a shop."

"Dat's right! Dat's right!" the girls shouted from all around in different dialects. "We got no work ourselves; we can't give them three days of our week. We don't make enough for our board these days!"

When the noise subsided, another girl stood up, a tall, pale-faced, very neat-looking person.

"What I want to ask you is this" — she turned to the last speaker. "What if the boss did not close that shop? Would there be more work? He closed it for his benefit, not for yours. How would you like to stay out of a job? What I say is this — we should divide as much work as there is among all of us. It is not fair, it is selfish to think only of yourself in such bad times. I make a motion to take it to a vote, and any girl who has any common sense and any feelings will vote right!"

All that time the girls of the other shop were sitting quietly in one corner, restlessly waiting for the decision. Their faces turned pale when the first girl began to speak. Now they were looking up disgustedly, waiting for the vote to be over.

"Let's have a secret vote," some one suggested.

"Why, are you ashamed to say 'no' in the open?" a girl of the other shop inquired sarcastically.

"A secret vote, a secret vote," a few more suggested.

But I refused them.

"You shall not have the closed vote. If you are not ashamed to act against those girls, you shall not be ashamed to do so in their presence. I want you to think it over for a few minutes. Don't do to others what you would not like them to do to you.

"Now, all who are in favor of having the other shop with us, please raise your hands."

My heart slowly went down, when hands went up. I counted. Sixteen hands, while there were over a hundred girls.

"Against," I stammered. Up went hands, many, many hands. It seemed to me they were unconsciously destroying something so very dear, something so very noble, something which thousands of workers are bitterly fighting for, are sacrificing their lives for, — UNITY, EQUALITY, and JUSTICE!

I sank in my chair full of embitterment. I felt as if they had pronounced a verdict of "starvation" upon those girls, and I felt ashamed, ashamed to look up at them.

"Am I allowed to say something?" came a voice from the corner, and up rose a worker of the other shop — a girl of about twenty-seven, with big, deep-blue, round eyes, hollow cheeks, nicely shaped but bloodless lips, a well-formed nose, and above all, a wealth of beautiful blonde hair, which framed her delicate and one-time beautiful face. She was on the committee and I knew her well. I was very much interested in her. She was only twenty-seven, and everybody spoke of her as of a passed beauty, as if she were forty. I often thought of her, and through my own experiences I well imagined what a hard life she must have had being a shopgirl, when, with all her heart and soul, she protested against the exploitation of the miserable wage-earners.

"You have the floor now," I said.

"Chairlady and *dear friends,*" — she pronounced the last words sarcastically, "I did not want to speak before you gave out your decision, so as not to sway your mind. I wanted you to act with your own clear conscience. Now, when all is over, allow me to tell you something: I'm nine years in this country, nine years in the same trade, and for nine years I had not one happy day. Few of you know what a shop of eight or nine years ago was like; few of you here remember how we worked at that time: sixty and seventy hours a week in sweat-shops — sweat-shops worse than hell! For nine long years I fought against such hell; for all these miserable years, I, together with so many others, went on agitating, explaining in what hell we lived. We wanted to live like human beings; we wanted to be treated like human beings; we wanted to be united, to be on friendly terms, to work in solidarity, — for solidarity, my friends, was at that time a thing unimaginable.

"In need of money, the workers would hunt for a bigger share of work, often bribing the foreman of the place, or any one who had charge of giving out work. In smaller places, where the boss himself took charge, they worked for less than the others, in order to get more work. One competed against another, and each considered the other an enemy. And *we*, for organizing the workers, were fired from the shops, and it took us weeks until we were able to find other jobs, only to be thrown out again in a short time. A great many of us were black-listed, and were not able to find jobs at all. We have suffered — suffered with the hope that we will gain in the end. That was nine, six, and even four years ago.

"Now, when we have a union of nearly two thirds of the industry, when we have a so-called 'Protocol of Peace' and other agreements with the bosses to protect the workers, we — the active, loyal union members — are not much better off. We are still thrown from the shops.

"True, the bosses are not as free to fire us as they were a few years ago, but they are applying all sorts of schemes to get rid of the active members. The first year after the last strike, conditions were all right. The workers were enthusiastic, and the employers saw that they dealt with united people, but little by little, the workers cooled off. They thought that by having the protocol they would be protected, and ceased paying their dues, ceased to attend shop meetings, where they could get fresh impressions. They ceased to take part in the shop activities. They left everything to one chairlady. The employers soon noticed their indifference and took advantage of it — they began to cut down prices, violate minimum scales, violate hours of labor as in the 'good old times.' The active members protested, and their lives were made miserable.

"Ask any one of us here, and she'll tell where she came from. One lost her job for being on the price committee; another for being chairlady; still others lost their jobs because their firm closed up the shop, giving out the work to contractors who get cheap help. This season, that has been so bad for the entire industry, affected us the worst. For the last four months, we had no more than six weeks of work, and mostly all of us have to support families. Some must help their families who were the first war sufferers. We went into debt, with no idea when we would be able to repay. What are we to do now? We know that you also earned very little, but little is better than nothing in time of a crisis. If we had acted before as you did now, we would have kept our jobs. If we did not care for you, and had accepted lower wages, what would you do now? You would have stayed out now! But we sympathized with you; we considered you our sisters, and did not want to injure you. We fought for equality, we fought for a better life, and if we had no sympathy from our employer it was because we interfered with his business. But to have no sympathy from you is a shame, shame! With your actions, you discourage all union feelings. Others in our place would surely scab on you!

"You leave us now, and don't care, because you cannot feel what it means to go around idle. Shame! Shame! You are an ignorant lot. You are ignorant!" She stopped, her mouth foaming, her eyes burning with excitement.

They all stood up at once. "Shame! Shame!" suddenly broke out in a roar of voices, deafening the room. I fell back on my chair, weakened with exhaustion. That was a cry full of protest, a cry of disgust, a fearful cry of hungry, starved, wronged voices. An army of girls, who create wealth, ready and willing to do the best for the world; and the world for them? — nothing!

CHAPTER XXI

DOWNHEARTED, broken with disappointment, my mind confusedly wandering, I dragged myself home. Is this what I have been working so hard for, giving away my entire time for the workers in my shop, developing in them the spirit of unity, of brotherhood and sisterhood — But, after all, are they to blame? They had not a full week's wages since the season started. They also lived in great want.

Oh, that eternal repetition — slack, busy; busy, slack! My head grew overburdened with heaping up broken thoughts. Justice, rights, wrongs, united force, organization, fight for equality, humanity — all these straight and crooked letters began to dance before my eyes, up and down and around, mingling together, losing shape and form. My head could not accommodate them freely and assort them coolly. Everything appeared to be a farce — this present world a farce, life around me a farce. Nothing was real. What's to-morrow, or a day after to-morrow? What is there in all these coming days and months? Where is the solution of misery? Where — where? Does it pay to live, after all? Work, work, and never earning enough for a living! Eternal worry — how to make ends meet.

Work in theory is noble. It is praised by poets, priests, and high authorities. I believe in the nobleness of work, and want to work, but I also believe that those who work are worthy of the rewards of their labor; those are the ones worthy of respect and admiration. But if we do not get that, does it pay to work? If I am not able to find justice, what do I want to live for? Does it pay to live? Does it pay? —

As those hopeless thoughts kept on pouring into my mind, I discovered myself watching the gas-lamp, its pipe circling over the table.

I was all alone in my room; alone in my silent emptiness. In the stillness of the evening how easy it would be just to put the pipe into my mouth, one, two, three minutes, and then anguish will die away. No more will my heart be gnawing, no more will I rack my brains, no more will my soul cry out in despair; free will my spirit be from the clutches of misery, free of that gnawing, gnawing pain of injustice — one — two — three — and a cold, lifeless body will stretch on the floor. It will be buried somewhere in a lonely place, and soon — very soon — the worms will eat into the flesh until nothing will be left. Br-r-r — what an ugliness! What an ugliness!

But what difference does it make — worms eating my flesh or human exploiters eating my freedom, my youth, my strength, my happiness —

one — two — three, and all will end. No more will I see the workers toiling, no more will I see them starving, no more will I fight for human conditions — but no, how can I do it? I dare not deprive them of my life; my parents in the war country, my little sisters, my brothers in the cursed war; they do not want me to die. They need me, they want me to live — But why do I need parents, and brothers and sisters, to worry about them? Who imposed them all on me? Would it not be better if I had none of them, if I was alone, belonging all to myself, and had no duties to anybody? Why should I live and suffer, just because my death will hurt my parents? Why can't I shake off all the misery, all the pain that possesses me? Why can't I die when that will relieve *me?*

But another voice, strong and severe, full of reproach, rose within me, and awakened me from my dark brooding. I stood up, but my head bent down with heaviness, my body was feeble, and I fell back half fainting —

I was startled with a feeling of something very cool on my forehead, and opened my eyes. Near me stood Ida, one of my shopmates, holding her cold hand on my forehead and watching me anxiously.

"How did you happen to come here?" I inquired in surprise.

"Why, you poor kid, I seen you at the meeting

this afternoon. You did not look like yourself at all. You was so nervous, irritated, and pale, like a ghost. Well, I thought to myself, something is the matter with her, but I ain't going to ask her, for it's none of my business; so I went home. But I worried about you and could not eat my supper, so I came to see what you was doing. I been watching you for ten minutes now. You was breathing so heavy and your face was so unhappy, that I thought you have a very bad dream, so I put my hand on your head to wake you — What's the matter with you? Are you sick?" she inquired anxiously.

"No, Ida, I don't think I'm sick. How late is it, please?"

"It's already seven o'clock."

"Only seven!" I wondered; "it seems as if it were a long, long time since I last saw you at the meeting. Sit down near me, Ida, and talk to me a little. I don't know what's the matter with me these days, but I seem to fall into such peculiar moods. A sea full of absurd thoughts is constantly arising in my mind. They envelop my brain, they begin to rebel, deafening my ear with their noise. This weakens me so that I grow unconscious for a while. It is happening so often that, really, I'm afraid I should lose my mind altogether."

"Oh, stop that nonsense. I, too, was feeling so bad once upon a time. It's nothing but loneliness.

I remember, when I used to come home from work so tired and there was n't nobody to give me as much as a smile. From all the trouble that I used to have in the shop, I used to come home and put my head in the cushion and cry the whole evening. I lived with strangers, and strangers don't bother much with you. But since I got married, it's all over. You see, I did not care for money. I love my husband and we are both working. We furnished a little apartment, and now I got my own little home, and somebody who likes me and thinks about me, I'm not lonely any more. I tell you, you ought to get married, take it from me. You're lonely, that's all the matter with you."

I smiled at her authority. How naïve she seemed. She really believed that I was nothing but lonely, and all I needed was to get married.

"Does nothing else worry you, Ida? The shop, its conditions, the surroundings, your work?" I asked.

"Oh, well, what good will it do me if I worry? What can we workers do? Take my word — it does n't pay to worry. I can't change this world. We make our living somehow." (As an operator on waists she was extremely quick and always made more money than the average worker. Among the two hundred of our workers there were only five or six who were so quick, and in busy time, they could make good money. Now, in slack time, she tried to get along on her husband's scanty earnings.)

"What would you do, Ida, if you had a child and could not go to work? Would your husband's wages be sufficient for you?"

"I should say not," Ida retorted. "But I ain't going to have no children until my husband can make enough for us."

"Bless you, Ida," I said approvingly. "Oh, how I wish that all those miserable wage-earners should stop breeding human stock until they can abolish poverty, until they can abolish slums, until they can make their government provide for them a human standard of living and treat them like worthy citizens; for no government, no country, can ever exist without workers. The workers are the basis of a rich country, they are the creators of all the wealth, and they are to be benefited by their work. I think if all the workers of all the trades and industries agreed to refuse to have children — this would be the most successful strike. If they only would refuse to have children, until human beings are considered higher than money, and too good for dirty slums!"

"I t'ink so, too, but do you believe this will ever happen? Eh, you foolish dreamer!" Ida replied kindly. "Now, until your workers will stop bringing children, won't you have something to eat? I'll bring you up anything you like to get."

She went down, and was back in a few minutes.

"A gentleman is asking for you," she said breathlessly.

"Oh, yes, a friend of mine. I forgot all about the appointment I made with him for this evening. Tell him to come right in."

"Oh, I see," she retorted significantly, and went to open the door.

My friend entered, slightly alarmed at my condition. He was an old admirer of whom I had lost track over a year ago, when he suddenly left town, and I never heard from him until he had recently returned. From our conversations since his return, I discovered that he purposely disappeared from my sight, so as to give me time enough to think, and now he came back to assure himself of the hopes that he cherished for two years. I liked him, and had much sympathy for him, but as his earnest pleas to answer his love became too frequent, I grew tired of his presence and tried to avoid him. I was therefore amazed to feel that I received him rather with a gleam of joy that evening. What made me feel so pleased, I did not understand.

Ida immediately found herself a third party. She put her hat on and under the pretence that her husband was lonely, she told us good-night, her eyes twinkling meaningly at me.

"Lisa, what happened? Are you sick?" he inquired anxiously, sitting beside me when the door closed behind Ida. "Something is surely the matter with you. I wish so much I could comfort you and relieve your pain. You need a rest. You need to leave the city. You need to be out of the noise. Why not come with me —"

And on he went, making proposals, working out plans, promising to do everything in his power to make me happy.

I sat silently listening to him, and as he pictured to me the happiness of our future married life, I began to feel a little agitated by his illusions, but that was only an impulse. I realized immediately how absurd it was. It could never be as he imagined, because he was a poor, exploited wage-earner; but more because I did not love him.

It was only a short time after the other shop was given up, when we, too, were left without work. We were now assembled in the shop every day, eagerly waiting for bundles that might by chance come in. The boss suggested that we reduce our prices on labor, so that he might get some orders at a cheaper rate. That we refused to do, for we knew the bitter results following the reductions in prices.

Weeks wore on, and no orders came in. We were already tired out with the dulness, and with fear we met each new-coming day that brought us no work. Having nothing to do, we would gather in groups near our machines and tell our troubles — the main theme being the war. Nearly all had families or relations either in Poland, Lithuania, or Galicia, who were ruined by the war, and whom these girls had to help. Until now, they had deprived themselves of necessities and shared their scanty earnings with their unfortunate relatives, but now there was nothing they could share. Their own board and rent were not paid, and even their car-fare was often borrowed.

Our boss also was very restless and we perceived that something was to happen soon. And so it did. He announced, with great regret, however, that the shop would close up — so the firm decided. From a long conversation with him, I learned that he also was a victim of the firm.

They had saved him from bankruptcy once, and took him into partnership, buying his name. Now, after one year of partnership, they were pushing him out without his name!

"I'd never thought they'd double-cross me so," he said bitterly.

Indeed, the other bosses acted meanly against him. Of all of them he was the fairest and they did not like him for it. They thought he was too good to the employees and that was against their principles.

I was very sorry for my boss, who was one of the very few who did not oppose workers' union, but still more sorry that the shop closed up, for we knew that the firm would reopen it soon with other workers, unorganized and cheaply paid.

Sure enough, the shop was moved to another district, and reopened the next month, with only a few of the old workers, mostly those who were never brave enough to express their discontent. All of us who were loyal union members and stood for our rights were never taken back. This was a method very much in style with the manufacturers to get rid of active members. They called it reorganization of their business, and as the employers have a right to reorganize, we were often helpless against them.

My search for work began as soon as our factory closed. There were now armies of us going around idle and we saw few prospects of getting more work. But I got into the habit of wandering around, and each morning a precious nickel brought me downtown, where I paced the city streets, absent-mindedly.

Swamped in that unemployed army of half-starved, worn-out working-girls, I gradually underwent a change. I no more experienced that shuddering fear against slack and starvation as in the former seasons. I seemed to have grown accustomed to it. Instead of fear, I felt disgust, and I became hardened with apathetic indifference; my room and books lost all interest for me. I had not read a book in weeks. Morning and evening I wandered around peeping into bright corners of Broadway, gay entrances to cabarets, through which crowds were constantly pouring, to plunge and whirl in the wild, blustering orgies of carnality. I peeped into the dark, dirty Bowery slums, into the infested-with-white-slavery Fourteenth Street — in fact I peeped everywhere, often with carelessness, often with sheer curiosity.

There were two things that still stirred my blood and painfully pierced through my heart and soul. They were the bread-lines and the flourishing traffic in live souls that is so openly performed in the streets of a city with high moral laws!

I more than once watched the bread-line, in cold, often stormy evenings, when the long row of shabby, half-naked beggars cuddled up, pressing tight to each other to protect themselves against the wind, stamping energetically with their feet, going through all sorts of contortions to warm themselves, while waiting through the long hours until a door would open at last and a "generous hand" would endow each one in turn with a dry bread-crust and watery cup of coffee.

I saw another bread-line one night up at Eleventh Street, where no coffee, only dry bread and scoldings were given. Six men happened to be late and the old man who gave out the bread frowned at them.

"You lazy things, — don't you know that if you want to get bread you must come in line at ten o'clock. I counted only fifty, and cut bread for that many. Now you'll have to wait till to-morrow."

One of the six silently slipped out of the line, and as I followed him, he stopped near a restaurant hungrily watching the inviting food display in the window. I approached him and put ten cents into his palm. His eyes filled with tears as he looked at me in surprise, and clutched my hand with a silent, expressive gratefulness.

When I returned to the line, the old man brought out some dry slices of bread and gave it to the others, saying: "Plenty of wurk. Why don't you find something to do? I'm also an old man, and I wurk twelve hours a day. You are too lazy to wurk, too lazy even to stand in line. Oh, you!"

They silently accepted the scolding, just as they silently came and waited, and in silence they walked away.

As I stood watching the line, I questioned the old man. He admitted that many of them had to be taken care of.

"It's the liquor, it's all that liquor that brings them down," he said regretfully.

I looked into their faces, — there were drunken bums, old, feeble men, and other life-stamped wretches, — odds and ends of one-time blooming bodies. And the old man's reproach — "Why don't you wurk?" — sounded ironical to me.

How can they work — who will employ them? They were driven out of employment by younger and more vigorous workers. And if they do happen to get employment, they get the "dirtiest work" there is to be done. No wonder they drop it soon. But even if they are lazy — laziness is a sickness and it must be cured, and cured carefully.

I looked at that useless "stock" and the painful question rose loudly in my heart, Who is guilty of those people's wretchedness, of their laziness? —

They were young once, and with their work they did contribute something to society, and it's the fault of the structure of society that they became useless. Society is responsible for spoiling them, society must provide for them. A home for such people could be built and kept with very little cost. How can people, with the least spark of human feeling in them, enjoy their wholesome, plentiful food in a warm, comfortable home, when not so far from them, out in the cold, old, sick, thinly clad people are waiting for a piece of dry bread? How can they?

Still, you see, on one side, people in brightly lighted hotels and gay cabarets, lavishing hundreds and thousands of dollars for wine and food, two thirds of which goes into waste-barrels, and on the other side — people waiting twenty-four hours for a dry bread crust, which they are not able to chew. Poodles and bulldogs are kept in luxurious apartments, and human beings are lucky if the policeman does not chase them off the hard benches of Cooper Square, where they find their lodging for the night. Oh, that scene of the stretched-out beggars on the benches would fill me with rage, and I was ready to call out to them, "Come, let's break into those spacious, beautiful homes; there is enough room for everybody!"

I more than once watched young girls go through the glaring streets, trafficking with their honor. The purity of womanhood was so shamelessly, vulgarly trampled upon in front of the hypocritical "moral watchers" who seemed to turn their heads away purposely so as not to notice that which everybody else so well noticed. I would thrill with aversion at such permitting of the ugliest of ugly deeds. My heart and soul would tremble with indignation for my sex — and again that burning question, Who is guilty of such an ugly stain spread upon humanity? Who is guilty of the ruin that is brought upon many a family through such shame?

I came to witness many disastrous cases in my close touch with the struggling world. How many families must have been ruined through such shame, I thought, as I watched those girls lurking about the streets. How many more victims will low wages and the present unemployment contribute to the market of shame? Who is guilty, and why are not men equally prosecuted for that vice?

With lingering pain in my heart, I would return home from my adventures. Never before had I seen so much misery and ugliness, for never before had I had courage enough to look so close into the dirtiest, vilest districts of the city in which thousands of children — future American citizens — were raised. My curiosity, with which I started out on my adventures, disappeared. The more I studied life around me, the more I saw the desperate struggle of the deprived ones, the stronger my convictions grew, the clearer I saw that monstrous, capitalistic power — the power that causes misery, horror, and destruction to us; the power that builds its own happiness by robbing thousands of others of their happiness. And it was painful to realize that here, in this free democratic government, such crime — such individual anarchy — is so absolutely legalized.

My own circumstances were nullified in comparison with what I saw of others, and I grew less concerned with myself. My income for the last five months averaged about five dollars a week, while the New York State Factory Investigating Committee stated that nine dollars a week is necessary as a minimum wage for a working-girl. I now lived with a friend of mine, who was also out of work, and together we succeeded to drag out our existence. My friend's husband kept a second-hand furniture store, and were it not for the war, they might have been fairly prosperous. Second-hand furniture is mostly bought by new immigrant families, but since the outbreak of the European war, immigration has stopped and together with it the second-hand furniture sales. It went so far that my friend had to borrow money to pay rent for the unsold furniture. The only advantage my friend had of the store was the display of furniture from which — even though second-hand — she very often picked out quite artistic things to furnish her apartment. And we really had a very comfortable little home. I was particularly fond of the library, furnished with simple but artistic furniture, a lamp with a nice green shade that spread a soft pleasant light over the room, some cheap copies of famous pictures hung on the wall, and two plants at the corners completed the charm of the room, in which the feminine touch of my little romantic friend was felt on everything.

In the days of miserable disappointments, in the days of hunger, my friend was quite a tonic to me. I was often pleasantly surprised at that woman, with hardly any education, but such a strong intellect. We would both rejoice in the green, soft light of our library after a "sumptuous meal" of bread and herring — having Maeterlinck for our dessert. Maeterlinck was my friend's favorite, and in the bitterest moments, when her sufferings would reach the climax, she often said, with a little smile, "Well, well, it could be no worse than it is now, but as long as there is still a piece of bread, and some tea in the house, and Maeterlinck to carry me away high — high above the misery, I can hope patiently and search for my blue bird."

Our regular menu was bread, herring, and tea or coffee. I also discovered another sort of economy. Sitting in Central Park on a lonely day, I watched a child feeding squirrels with peanuts. The squirrels confidingly picked the peanuts from the children's palms, then ran away a few yards, dug a little hole in the ground, hid their fortunes, and returned for more, to the children's great delight; they jumped and whistled with joy at the squirrels' tricks. That play attracted me and I also bought peanuts for the squirrels. I was hungry, so I also treated myself to some peanuts and was surprised to feel that the lingering pain of hunger disappeared. From that day on, I tricked my stomach with peanuts. Whenever I walked around all day looking for work, and getting no food, I would still my hunger with peanuts, which certainly were economical. A nickel's worth of peanuts carried me around a whole day, and that gave me the courage to reject jobs that were sometimes offered to me for seventy-five cents a day. I was, and still am, strongly determined to live on peanuts, or not live at all, but never to sell my energy for seventy-five cents a day, never allow others to deprive me of my returns for my hard labor.

CHAPTER XXII

THE wheels of time kept turning on, speeding and grinding the dreary days and months — and so another year had gone by. The war was still going on, its flame embracing more and more nations. If it brought prosperity to the American financiers and munition-makers, it brought sorrow and pain to us. Some trades that depended largely on imports were actually crippled. It also affected our industry, and the workers suffered greatly from it.

Tired out from the long months of unemployment, the workers hastened to secure employment at the beginning of the year under any conditions provided by the employer. Now more than ever the employers took advantage of the workers' weakness; they trampled on our rights and ignored the agreement with the union.

What were we to do? A great many of us who refused to work below the minimum, travelled from one shop to another, until we finally had to accept a lower wage. Our union suffered a sore crisis. In the long weeks of unemployment, members ceased to pay dues, so that at the beginning of the year our treasury was nearly depleted. In order to bring back our members and help them become in good standing, and also to encourage unorganized workers to join our organization, the union gave out a manifesto, lowering the initiation fee from $5.41 to $2.41. That amount initiated a member into the union, and made a member in far arrears become in good standing.[1]

Little by little our union began to pick up, and was soon engaged in a desperate struggle to restore the standards which our employers had lowered.

If conditions due to the strike had improved in 1913, they grew worse in 1914 after the European War broke out, and became worse and worse. The employers paid low wages, claiming that times were bad, due to the war. Whether or not it was true, the fact was that the least little thing was ascribed to the war. The cost of living went on increasing from day to day, wages were small, and the workers had to carry all on their stooping shoulders.

We realized that it was necessary to modify the protocol and amend it, so as to make it more effective and bring it to the real object of its existence — that is, the establishment of "just and fair" standards of working conditions in the dress and waist industry, and to adjust the relations between employers and workers on a basis of fairness and helpfulness. We had had these attractive words for three years on the pages of the protocol, but we seldom had them in the shop.

[1] A union member who fails to pay his weekly dues for a period of more than eight weeks is not in good standing.

We held mass meetings and local meetings to invoke the workers' enthusiasm. A great deal of agitation was carried on by our "Gleichheit," a Yiddish weekly given out by our union to keep members informed of the conditions in the industry, discussing social and economic questions — also literature. Two more editions, one in English, the other in Italian, were given out for the convenience of our non-Yiddish-speaking members.

Our International Ladies' Garment Workers' Union, consisting of all the local unions of the ladies' garment industry, sent out special organizers all over to help organize the entire trade, not only in New York, but also in the vicinity, and in other cities. But the work was interrupted by a frame-up of anti-unionists and scab agencies which were assisted by a number of manufacturers. Twenty-three of our union representatives, the best, the most loyal to the cause, were indicted by grand juries on the testimony of gathered statements by a certain leader of a criminal gang, that our union leaders had hired gangsters to help them win strikes, and that they often caused violence or damage to the "innocent" employer. Eight of our leaders were accused of murder in the first degree, the rest of other crimes. That stirred up the entire organized world, also a number of laymen.

At the same time, as if purposely to break the union, the cloak manufacturers broke up their protocol agreement with the union. It would have resulted in a bitter strike, had not the mayor formed a council of conciliation which brought the two parties together and thus avoided a strike.

Meanwhile, our leaders waiting for their trials were kept in the Tombs. The organized workers who knew who the real hirers of gangsters were, bitterly resented such a shameful frame-up. With heart and soul they threw themselves into a struggle against those who were intent on wiping out our best and most able people.

And after many months of loud protests and exhausting strain, we succeeded in convincing the world that they were innocent, and in October, 1915, they were set free.

When all was over, our union began to make preparations to improve conditions in our trade. Our board of directors immediately began working on the modifications of the protocol and new demands, so as to present them to the Employers' Association.

Each new demand was carefully discussed and acted upon by special member meetings. Our mass meetings were successful; our workers showed great enthusiasm and understanding of the demands.

We demanded an increase in wages, and a forty-eight-hour week instead of fifty.

We were ready to declare a general strike if our demands were ignored. But the Employers' Association soon met our union in conference to discuss matters.

After many conferences, unable to agree, both parties submitted their disputes to the Board of Arbitration.

The association controlled only half the industry; the rest was in the hands of individual employers, some of whom had individual agreements with our union and some were not unionized at all. To make similar agreements with them and enforce equal standards throughout the industry, we had to call a general strike.

The exciting preparations then began. First, we organized the workers among whom we worked for the coming demonstration. Many of us were discharged from several places for doing it, I among them. But I did not care. I hoped that in the near future, through this new strike, we would gain better conditions, that the new agreement would forbid an employer discharging a worker for union activities, and so I was willing to suffer another few weeks.

The active members were assigned by the union to different committees, each performing an important duty. And we worked very hard. In rain or snow, we did not fail to meet and plan together. We were all anxious to plan right and do our bit for the success of the strike.

At last, on February 9th at two o'clock in the

afternoon, a red circular waved by a committee in each shop was the signal to the workers to stop. At the sight of the red circular thousands of workers stood up at the same minute, folded their work, put their aprons into the baskets and peacefully marched down. Crowds of them were pouring out from the different buildings into the streets, mingling together, greeting each other. Their happy cheers loudly echoing in the air were caught and enthusiastically answered by new groups who were constantly joining the crowd from the neighboring streets, and the avenues soon became black with the multitudes of the young toilers. Races, nationalities, were forgotten: Jews, Italians, Americans, Slavs, Germans, colored people — all combined together in one desire, a desire for a better life. On they marched, the crispy frost encouragingly crackling under their swift feet. Their happy cheers were like the remote, sweet bell-ringings of a glorious future, and my heart bubbled with emotion as I watched that live procession on the snow-clad February day.

I compared them with the many processions I witnessed so often in the early morning when the crowds were moving on to the monotonous toiling world. Those were mourning processions, dull, automatic movements of a down-trodden mass who carried all the thorns of life in their ignorant indifference.

But what a different procession I saw now. Multitudes moving on, but moving lively, — pale but happy were those young toilers who clothed the nation and themselves were shabby. Pride and dignity shone in their eyes. Happy were they when they left the factories, not to return until better conditions and fairer considerations will be granted to them. And in my heart I blessed them all, blessed their noble fight for a glorious freedom, blessed their craving for a human life.

The meeting halls especially provided for the strikers were soon overcrowded. Over thirty thousand workers were on strike, and we thus hoped to get in close touch with all of them — to explain to them the aims and accomplishments of our union, to advise them how to use our joint strength intelligently, how to look out for our rights, and not allow the employers to trample on us. We came close together with girls who had never had the courage to hope for better conditions and who now, under the influence of so many strikers, grew enthusiastic and hopeful, and demanded from their employers recognition of the union.

While the Board of Arbitration was still in session, the individual employers, with the exception of a few, came to the union office willing to sign contracts. (The season was already on. And since the employers knew that an agreement is only effective when the employees stand strongly and demand it together, and since they hoped to rid themselves of the brave and persistent workers as in the former days, and have their own ways — they were hastening to sign an agreement with the union so as to get back the workers and be on time with their orders.)

In the halls the committees in charge worked hard to keep the strikers enthusiastic and everything was conducted in an orderly manner, but a demoralization arose among the strikers in certain halls due to the misleading of some speakers from the ranks. There were a few members, quite intelligent persons and with good intentions, who caused some trouble with their speeches. Not being present at the special meetings at which our demands were discussed before the strike, they were ignorant of many facts, and, failing to realize that, entrusting our disputes to the Board of Arbitration, we had to accept its decision, unless it is absolutely against us, they appealed to the strikers not to make any compromises, not to accept any decisions from the Board unless all our demands were granted to us.

The Board of Arbitration did not grant us all our demands, but its decision as a whole was favorable, and though a great many of us were not quite pleased we accepted the conditions because we had agreed to arbitrate.

When the decision was brought to the strikers, those who were influenced by the appeals of the few not to compromise refused to accept it. They accused the representatives of the conference as acting autocratically by accepting the decision, but the clearer-thinking workers, who had carefully followed and studied the special meetings and also the sessions of the Board of Arbitration, were in full sympathy with our representatives, for they saw our strenuous efforts to get for the people whatever possible. With great difficulty we succeeded in restoring order among the discontented ones, and after one week, when also a great number of individual agreements were signed, the people gradually returned to work.

By little and little everything smoothed. After such a huge demonstration of over thirty thousand workers, things were slowly coming into shape. The last decision was given out by the Board, and the final modified agreement was drawn up.[1]

The protocol as it read appeared favorable if the employers would only carry out all that is provided for us as stated; and if instead of short seasons we had steady work; but above all, if the workers themselves would stand together, and all like one be on the lookout.

We returned to work with the hope that now,

[1] For those interested in the details, a condensed form of the agreement is attached at the end of this book.

with an increase in wages and a promise of fair and just relations between the employers and workers, our existence would improve. But three months have passed since the "new régime," and I stood without a job again. It was the middle of May now. This time I was not discharged, I left the shop myself. But I left it as I left some of my former jobs, where, having no grounds for discharging me, they made it so unpleasant that I was compelled to leave.

It was my eighth job since I returned to work after the strike. In a period of three months I worked in eight shops, five of which I left myself and from the rest I was discharged.

Why did I leave, and why was I discharged? As always, I was one of the few workers in the shop who demanded our union conditions, and not only for ourselves, but for the entire shop, and as such workers we were discriminated against and forced to leave.

If we did not find in our pay envelope the extra pay for overtime, or the minimum rate that was promised to us by the agreement, and we demanded it, we were called "kickers."

If we refused to work more than the regular hours, we were called "trouble-makers."

If we demanded preference to union workers — or if we protested against unfair treatment — we were called "God damn foreign anarchists." And what were we not called just because we demanded a living wage for our work!

When signing the protocol, our employers agreed to grant us in good faith all the provisions provided therein. If only they would have given us in good faith what belonged to us, we would have had nothing to object to — and would gladly have worked quietly.

But they did no such a thing. They gave us nothing in good faith. We had to fight for every bit in order to get it.

"Fair treatment" and "good faith" on the part of the employers remained nothing but beautiful phrases. In reality, they acted precisely as in the former days. They violated the agreement — some more, some less. And those of the workers who protested against violations, who demanded what was coming to them, were purposely treated badly as a punishment for their activity or sent away altogether.

A great many such workers, having gone through a great deal of suffering because they tried to help their fellow workers, would finally grow disgusted and cease their activity in order to avoid the employers' persecutions. They would lose hope of ever expecting justice from their employers, and with embitterment and hate they would settle down to work, accepting everything quietly, — wishing and praying that a miracle (either through marriage or something else) might happen and save them from the shop.

Our union fought discriminations against active members, and often helped them to retain their positions, but I seldom complained to the union to protect my job. I was too indignant to work for an employer who did not want to employ me, and who, not being able to discharge me for my union activity, would give me work as one would throw bones to a dog. I was too indignant to remain in such places — and left to look for another job. And thus, leaving shop after shop, I worked in forty different places through my entire career as waist-maker.

In most of the factories where I worked, they found me desirable enough until I asked for a living wage, or until my fellow workers demanded a square deal. My fortieth job I decided should be the last. I could not stand it any longer. When in my last shop our boss wanted us to work the first of May, — which our union has always celebrated by a demonstration, appealing to all union members to join them in the march, — they called a shop meeting, and at the meeting I spoke to the workers and made them realize that it would be unfair if we did not respond to the union's call; and if we did work for our employer, it would be unfair to those employers who allowed their workers to stop that day. Our workers agreed with me and stopped from work the first of May. But after that day the forelady began to put me back in my work. She would make me wait a long time for the least particle of the work; she would also leave my questions unanswered. When I asked for an explanation, she broke out in a shower of fury: —

"You got the nerve, to expect me to treat you right, when we wanted the girls to come in Monday [the first of May] and you threatened them to stop! You think we don't know that you try to influence the girls to make us trouble — you think if you got a union, you are not afraid to be fired! Union lady! We don't want such people as you — you spoil us all the girls! —"

I cut her short.

"If only you had told me that the first day, instead of keeping me back in my work, I would have saved you the trouble. I assure you that though I have a union, I will not fight for the job. But what I want you to know before I leave is that I never did such a thing as threatening. We had a full right to stop from work when the workers in the other shops stopped, and we were no exception.

"Just as Independence Day, or Washington's Birthday, or Lincoln's Birthday is dear to any patriotic American, and to me, too, so is the first of May — as an International Labor Holiday — dear to me, and I had a right to speak and explain to the girls the significance of it. You say I spoil the girls — why? Because I tell them to complain to the union when you fail to pay them double for overtime! Because I try to acquaint them with the details of the protocol, of which they are ignorant, and of which they should know! You don't like to see people who understand and who can see what's wrong. Well — as for myself — I shall relieve you. I shall not stay and be at your mercy, that you should give me work whenever you desire, not when I need."

And I left the shop.

I worked in forty factories — Independent Union shops, Association shops. To each factory I came ready to perform my work, and with hope of earning a living wage. But the conditions in the shops compelled me to protest, and if I — like many others — lost faith of ever expecting justice from our employers, I did not settle down to work in dull hopelessness. I never learned to become the "worker who ought to be glad to get employment." No, I was never content just with getting employment — I wanted something else. I wanted to be paid enough for my work so as to get sufficient good food to supply me with sufficient physical energy; a nice, airy, comfortable room to rejoice and rest in after a day's hard work; enough clothes to keep me clean and also keep me warm in cold weather; enough time for rest, recreation, and above all, for spiritual development. — God knows how we crave it!

All this is necessary to keep one in good health and spirits, to keep one contented and desirous to work. I am not only desirous, I am eager to work in order to live and enjoy life. But I refuse to live in order to work! Life in itself is so attractive, so full of blessings, that I refuse to let it slip through my hands. I refuse to stand aside and let my mouth water while watching others enjoy it in full.

There were some employers who did recognize our rights to live. They advised us to apply to charity for aid. I recall once arguing with a boss about a girl cleaner — she was seventeen years of age, self-supporting, and received only five dollars a week. I tried to explain to him the needs of a girl of her age. He listened to me attentively and said: "But, my dear, you should not appeal for sympathy in a business place — this is no charity institution. In here I am concerned with business only! I donate enough to charities, and — if you say the girl cannot live on what she gets — there are enough charity homes for working-girls, where they can live on small wages."

Through my experiences in dealing with employers, I heard that from many of them, who hope that charity will take care of their workers. Nothing could provoke me more than this. They wanted us to work for them, and for our own living they wanted us to beg, to ask for charity. — Oh, how I hated the word charity! The mere mention of it sounded to me as a humiliation to mankind!

We do not want charity! We do not need any! We want what belongs to us for our labor, we want it in full!

CHAPTER XXIII

IT was Saturday when I left my shop — the middle of May when the dull season is already rapping on the door.

I came home weary, not so much from the argument with the forelady as from physical weakness. During the general strike I was on the Hall Chairman's Committee, having charge over a hall, and keeping the strikers. in order. Speaking all day long to strikers, I grew hoarse and caught cold, and while running around from one meeting hall to another, thinly clad in bad weather, my cold developed into influenza. That nasty cold gripped me for the third winter, and as I never had a chance to take care of it, a chronic nasal catarrh developed in a most severe form. Sneezing fits would keep me awake through the nights, making my life miserable. It caused me severe headaches, and my eyes would be moist with tears. But I never had time to think of it. My daily existence was made so hard for me; my shifting from one shop to another never gave me a chance to save up a few dollars, either for doctors' bills or for a warm coat that could prevent me from catching cold. Mentally and physically underfed, I grew thinner and paler every day, but strange though it was, my ill health had not interfered with my work. I had grown so used to my machine that I worked it automatically, with no special effort. It was only after work that I would be overtaken with fatigue, and would slowly drag myself to my lonely lodging-room. I lived now in an extremely small room in a shabbily furnished house, paying ten dollars a month. For such a room I had paid six dollars a month only three years ago.

Small, shabby, and also smoky from the little gas stove that I kept to make my own breakfasts and lunches, it was unfriendlier and shabbier still when I returned home that Saturday. The walls and ceiling hung low over my shoulders as black wings. My senses were twisted in dark hopelessness, for I had to look for work on Monday and, oh, how I hated it!

Forty shops, forty different places in four years! How many more years do I need for the completion of my brilliant shop career? And what is there to expect in the end? How much longer will I have to be scolded, insulted, humiliated, and managed by greedy bosses and stupid foremen? How many more pounds of flesh and blood must I lose at work? How many more darkest days must I walk through to reach the light of a new life?

And the stifling smoke in my room from the buttered frying-pan and burning eggs made the decision. Not a day longer under the present conditions! I would no more return to the shop, though to-morrow threatened with starvation. But was it a threat, after all? Had I not starved, had I not lived part of my time on the smell of food rather than on food itself? And food was not all. I was starved spiritually, had been starved for four long miserable years. Was I not deprived of everything, even though I worked? What was the use to continue work?

I sat at my dining-table, the little square table that served as desk, study-table, ironing-board, and everything else. My meal was untouched. I had no appetite, and nobody else would, being tired as I was and having to prepare the meal, sitting at the table with nobody to exchange a thought, eat in silence, and clean up afterwards. I looked about the room, at my food, at the newspaper that served as tablecloth, and unwillingly I heaved a deep sigh. What were my accomplishments for the four years? For the moment I pitied myself. And once more my early recollections rose with reproach and made me homesick.

I longed for my home with my devoted family, I longed for my early days surrounded with friends. I longed to be once more the ambitious "schoolmistress" surrounded by her pupils — sweet little girls with staring eyes, questioningly fixed on their teacher. If I could but see them once more around me delighted over some explanation! If I could once more play with them in the woods, looking into their dear, glowing little faces when they begged teacher to sing for them! Oh, if I could now fall asleep and, as often in my sleep, live again in those days and forget that for four years I have been nothing but a "Say!" and a "Listen!" and an "I want you!" and a "Who are you, anyway?" and a "kicker," and a "fresh thing," and a "God damn foreign anarchist" (that I never was). If I could but forget all the humiliations and return to my old days, which, though very unhappy because of the Government's brutality to us, though unendurable at that time, still after four years of American life, seemed the happiest. They were in truth very unhappy days, but at least I found solace in one cherished hope of running away to free America. But where was I to run now? Where should I look for my freedom now? — And I had no more hopes.

Mechanically my mind was making a review of my four years of American life, and I sank brooding over painful details.

Only four years ago I had left my home, unregretful of my step. I ran away from a country which tyrannized over our lives, which locked our brains and ambitions. I ran because my soul yearned in anguish for a free life, and I followed the magic lure of Freedom. I ran to the land of liberty. I came here young, hopeful, with vigor and blooming health. I was eager to become a member of a free nation, live among free people, serve in whatever way I could for the comfort and welfare of a free people, and get in return to drink from the full cup of that balsamic drink of Freedom.

But what did I find? In Russia I had time, but no freedom; here I had freedom, but no opportunity to enjoy it. I was made a slave, I was made to work hard for a mere existence. And where was there time for the free schools, for more knowledge, where was there time for the wonderful libraries, for the luxurious museums? Where was the opportunity to rejoice in all the blessings of this free country?

If we rejoiced in one thing, we did it at the expense of another. At the expense of our sleep we went to the library; at the expense of a few dinners we went to opera; at the expense of a better room we bought a dress; at the expense of our leisure we did our laundry; at the expense of a necessary walk we read a book.

We worked, worked, and our profits went into the hands of others. — And should this go on forever? — Why? — Why? — For four years I worked, I strove, I hoped, I struggled, I rebelled; after each new disappointment I would patiently brace up and take up life anew. But now after four years I was too tired to rebel any more, I was no more physically fit to endure such a life. My health was entirely broken. Four years of my best youth and physical strength I lost in my struggle for a better life, and had accomplished nothing. — What was the use of struggling any longer? In place of the one-time healthy, cheerful, ambitious girl, there stood now a stripped shadow — stripped physically — stripped economically. And should this stripped shadow, this already good-for-nothing wretch, go on living this life forever? Changing shops, demanding living wages and being thrown out for it, should she go on living in this miserable room, and forever starve for real life, or should she settle down to work in that dull, contented hopelessness like some of her fellow workers did in the end, raise no voice, accept the employer's terms, leave everything to his free will? It might be a little more profitable than to protest against injustice and fight for better conditions.

But stripped creature though I was, I decided to do neither. I said, "Enough of it! Either life in full or nothing at all."

Alone in my room I sat that Saturday afternoon, numb with hopelessness. In through the window the sun shone pleasantly; the soft, warm air brought whispers of spring into my tiny room. I had hardly noticed this spring coming at all. And only now I realized that it had nearly completed its duty and would soon be gone. It trimmed the earth with its luxurious freshness, spreading spicy fragrance. It brought the song birds to fill the air with merriment, it brought color and brightness into life. — And I — did I notice it? A gray autumn dimmed the windows of my soul, and its drizzling rain fell on my heart, freezing my hopes.

Hopes — oh, the beautiful hopes of my past! This new life in a free country has deceived and crushed us! What shall become of us now? How shall we begin our morrow? — And back and forth I paced, racking my brain trying to invent some plan that might help me change my life, but my wits failed me. The more I rambled in search for enlightenment, the deeper the darkness sat enfolding me into endless nights of uncertainty. The morrow stared with its unknown burdens, and shadows of fear spread around me dancing and teasing, roaring with hellish laughter.

My head dizzied, senses twirled, a rush of mad waves came heaving in my heart, shortening my breath, and tears came pouring, pouring endlessly, until pain was gone, leaving a blunt emptiness in my heart. I began to fear my own self, I feared the loneliness, I feared the narrow walls, and driven by fear I left my room in haste. I wandered in the squares and parks, I rambled for hours over the streets, cut and zigzagged with cold steel veins, and suddenly I felt lost amidst the noise and hurry-skurry. So many people around, and all strangers to me! Such a big spacious world and no place for me!

CHAPTER XXIV

I SLOWLY walked toward the Bar Association, where our Board of Arbitration held its session. I liked the Board, I liked its existence; for without strikes, without bloodshed, without losses to either side, but by peaceful means of careful consideration to their differences the Board often brought the workers and employers to an agreement. My experience in the end, however, shook my faith in it.

Silence reigned in the room when I entered and I tiptoed to the left side bordered with a cord, to divide it from the right where the employers sat. (Even there our bosses drew lines of distinction between us.) At one end of the room the Board presided. The chairman sat with his eyes half closed, leaning back in his chair, only the constant wrinkling of his high forehead showed his deep concern. The two arbitrators, one for the union and one for the employers, sat beside him, and with intent faces listened to the word-battles of the attorneys across the table.

The lawyer for the union spoke, and his well-trained voice, now falling, now rising, carried with force each new argument, strengthened the justification of our demands. But no less persuasive was the lawyer for the employers. With no less force did he repel our demands, not because they were unjust, but because he defended the interests of his clients who sat at the right listening to him. He defended their profits.

I sat among my tired pale sisters at the left, and from my seat I surveyed the "rights." For more than three years I had worked for them. I studied them, I knew them so well. I knew their attitude toward the Board — they hated it because it did not allow them to exploit the workers in the good old ways. They only tolerated the Board because they feared public opinion, but in their business establishments they more often ignored the Board's decisions. That was why the workers rose in protest; that was why a great many of them lost faith in the Board of Arbitration; that was why in return they too sometimes broke the rules of the protocol, thus violating the decision of the Board. And as I looked around me at the people, at the employers, at the arbitrators, their hard efforts and tireless energy to create new rules, new laws for the improvement of working conditions, seemed useless to me. They will not be observed anyway, for good working conditions mean less profit, and who has once tasted profit will not give it up so easily. And even if the employers of our industry did live up to the union agreement, would that solve our problem? I am not concerned with our industry alone; I see and feel the struggle, I hear the desperate cry against poverty and misery of all the toilers of the industrial world, and my problem is no more my own; it is national! It is for the nation's caretakers, for the upholders of American traditions to see that her children who build, enlarge, enrich the country, shall reap the fruit of their labor, shall enjoy the equality and liberty provided by this democratic country, shall be safeguarded from usurpers and parasites.

O, if only they cared enough, what a wonderful world we might have! And at those thoughts of beautiful possibilities new happy visions surrounded me.

I saw industry belonging to the people and for the use of the people, no more for the profit of the few. I saw the workers, not only building beautiful homes, but living in them too; I saw them emerging from slums and ignorance; I saw them straightening their stooping shoulders, raising their eyes with a proud, straightforward look; I saw them cleansing the streets from vice and crime, and transforming them into beautiful gardens blooming with love, equality, and brotherhood. I fluttered in the glory of a Future World, growing unconscious of my surroundings, when a gentle voice asking, "How is Lisa?" recalled me with a start to the present. I turned my head and met a radiant face with a row of smiling teeth:

one of my new friends, Juliet Pointz, greeted me warmly. I walked over and took a seat near her. Soon we were joined by another new friend, Robert Grosvenor Valentine, who had just been appointed head of the newly created Board to enforce the protocol standards. (The Board of Arbitration, realizing the difficulty in maintaining the standards for the workers in the shop, consented to the demand of the union to establish a Board of Control, in order to enforce the protocol conditions and equalize the standards throughout the industry. Unfortunately, neither the employers nor the union realized the full significance of such an establishment and the Board was terminated.)

I met Mr. Valentine often those days, as he was eager to get an insight into the shop and its effects upon our lives, and I readily answered his thoughtful questions. Through our long, intimate talks we soon became friends.

I feel greatly indebted to my friend, Miss Pointz, who introduced me to Mr. Valentine as one who understood the problems of our industry. It was through her that I gained the invaluable friendship of a real *true-spirited son of America.*

While Commissioner of Indian Affairs, Mr. Valentine instituted reforms for the welfare of the Indian, and vigorously prosecuted those who attempted frauds against the Indian tribes. As an industrial efficiency expert, he was not merely concerned with the material success of modern industry, but more with its effects upon the life of the worker, and his sudden death was not only a loss to his family and friends, but also a loss to the nation.

In a corner of the room the three of us sat, in the twilight of that fateful Saturday, and I tried to chat as if nothing had happened. But the blunt emptiness in my heart, that slowly changed into piercing anxiety as the realization of my present circumstances returned, must have shone through my eyes and betrayed me. My friend, Miss Pointz, looked at me anxiously and asked: —

"Well, what's the good news?"

"I am jobless again," I remarked, trying to be unconcerned.

"Jobless again — what is the matter with the girl?"

She knew of my activities and unwilling adventures and was not surprised at my announcement. They both teased me for continually shifting from place to place. But I found it hard to make light of it this time. I sat there painfully aware of the closing session, and that in another few minutes we would bid a friendly good-bye, and each would turn his own way. Where will *I* go, and what will I do? I feared so much to remain alone. But before I had time to decide, Mr. Valentine invited me to dinner. I was loath to return to my lonely room and was grateful for an invitation that would keep away my companion, anxiety, for at least another few hours.

We walked out and turned into Fifth Avenue swarming with the holiday crowd of a beautiful warm Saturday evening. On each corner we were urged to buy fresh violets and fragrant lilies-of-the-valley. After dinner we took a long, pleasant walk, accompanied by our usual discussions and disputes, and finally we turned into Washington Square and seated ourselves on a bench to rest and continue our talk.

"Tell me about your last job," said Mr. Valentine after a short silence.

I did tell him of my last job and also of my previous ones. He put questions now and then, and I was unconscious that he slowly drew out certain chapters of my life as I had lived it in the factories. Carried away by the flow of my own words, I went on telling him of the life of the multitudes, and the misery that reigned triumphantly in their homes.

"Come with me, and see for yourself," I said. And I led him through Fourteenth Street and other back streets flourishing with white slave traffic; down to Cooper Square where the homeless took possession of the hard benches for the night; and down through the narrow street, crowded with filthy tenements, where people lived and slept, and bred in misery or in happy ignorance a new generation, a new army for the industrial markets, for men are needed for industry, industry is for money, and money is needed for comforts, for luxuries, for lust, for vice, by the idle profiteers.

"But all that will disappear in time," he tried to argue. "Big profits must and will disappear in the end. Economic conditions are already improving."

"Oh, yes," I said; "a slight reform once in a long while, an increase of a dollar now and then. But do you know that as soon as we get that increase, the prices of food, clothes, and shelter spring up immediately, and our raise goes back to the profiteers. So you see that cannot abolish poverty with all its ugly consequences; and the burning question, 'What's to be done?' stands out again."

"Let us leave all these questions alone. Tell me what you intend to do now."

"What I intend to do?" I repeated. His question startled me with a jerk — it instantly brought me back to my reality. Quick as lightning memories of the past flashed through my brain, pointing to a hopeless future. I suddenly recalled my onetime, shrivelled forelady, her golden teeth that glared from her half-open, pitiful mouth, and a thrill of aversion ran through me. As yet I had no gold in my mouth, but I already shrivelled; oh, how I shrivelled! And that horrid vision brought forth a burst of agony, of words uncontrollable — I was not responsible for my answer.

"I have not the slightest idea, but I assure you back to the factory I shall not go. I see nothing awaiting me there. I have had enough, enough! — I have secured an insurance policy to provide for my family if things come to the worst; that is the best I can think of —" But that was as far as I went. The last words babbled out unconsciously brought me to realize that I spoke to a stranger, that my confession might invoke sympathy, but no, — sympathy was not so bad, — it was pity, pity, I hated. I felt ashamed and ridiculous and, oh, how I wanted my words back. But I was not given time to repent.

"Look here, 'Madame Pessimist,'" he said. "Now more than ever you must preserve your patience; the future is not so dark as you paint it."

"Yes, I see my future — stitching dresses, dresses, and more dresses!"

"Now, wait a moment, don't get the bad habit of interrupting people when they have something to say," he remarked; and continued: "I have listened to you for more than five hours now, and things you have told me have opened a new world to me, — not that I have not known of it, but, of course, I had the view of an outsider. I have never before heard it so clearly and fully put by one who has actually lived it. You have given me the most valuable information, and I shall need you to assist me in my future work. I want you to start, as soon as you are ready, to write about your experiences from your first shop and steadily on. I want all details, interesting or otherwise. Write of the work as it begins in the morning and ends in the evening. Write of the surroundings, the treatment, the relations between one worker and another, and between worker and employer. Write of their homes, their lives, their recreations, how it affected you and others."

I stared at him in utter bewilderment. For the moment I did not understand why he wanted all that — for what purpose.

"I shall begin very soon the investigation in this industry and your information will help to carry it on more successfully."

"But I can't write with my limited knowledge of English. I speak wretchedly enough, but my spelling — God help you! Spelling was always the most capricious of my friends, it demanded a great deal of my time that I never had."

"Do as I tell you; never mind the spelling; it is your brain I want to test. And so it is understood now, you are in my employ and I am to boss you whether you like it or not. You need not stay in the city, you can gather your tools — paper, carbon, pencil — and get off to the country where the atmosphere will inspire you to work. Every two days you shall have to send me your manuscript."

"Manuscript?" I stared again. "You don't

mean to make an author of me? I don't know how to write! No, thank you for the honor."

"I don't care what I make of you so long as I get my information."

I glared at him in a state of perplexity. What did it all mean? Why should a man whose acquaintance I had made only two months before, take the liberty of working out plans for me? I felt with sickening horror that not he was to blame, but I, whose silly tongue had let loose. "He simply desires to help you," a voice within repeated, and his suggestion humiliated me. I began to tremble with anger and shame at my weakness.

I could not realize that he really needed me, although his arguments were most convincing. He finally gave me his word of honor that he needed my service and added in his usual teasing way, "Now, go home, and don't you declare any more strikes on me."

I returned home. Tired and restless I sat up in my bed, leaning against the wall, my head seething with piercing doubts. To accept his offer or not? Would it be the right thing to do? Not to accept it — what else is there awaiting me? — voices kept on rising, gnawing my heart and soul. Oh, when will my heart stop aching? When will my soul find its rest?

Through my open window in the night-roofed,

mysterious darkness, light breezes came flowing in playing with my hair and caressing my face. They stirred my blood, infecting me with passionate desires to start out anew; to accept the chance that breaks open all doors of new possibilities. And visions, luring visions, surrounded me. Unheard sweet sounds, now jumping, now groping, now vanishing, and now returning, penetrated into the hidden depths of my soul, calling and singing, waking, luring me to a new start of life. My heart throbbed with ardor, the walls around me widened, the ceiling rose high, and out of the night the morning dawn arrived shining through the window brightening my soul. I slowly went to sleep under the unconscious murmurings — shall I? or shall I not? —

I did not so readily accept the offer. The next day found me very feverish and I hunted impatiently for some of my friends to seek advice. And Lord bless them! they all encouraged me, my friend Miss Pointz was delighted with the news.

"Why," she said, "I always felt that a thing like that should have been written about; you are lucky in having the chance, — make the best of it."

Not trusting my own common sense, but assured by others of the significance of the task, I at last accepted it, and the next days I walked as if in a trance.

Is it possible that I have escaped the factory — the institution of bondage? Is it possible that I am free now — no more a tool, no more a mere hand to move the machine? Is it possible that I can do something worthier than slave for profits? Is it possible that I shall no more be the slave of Want — that dreadful monster? Yes, all that was possible. For I was provided with a minimum wage now — a wage not based on the arguments of lawyers, but one based on my human needs!

And I began to work, supplying myself with paper, pencils, and half a dozen dictionaries, English, Russian, and Yiddish, for the task was not an easy one. Each sentence was thought out in Russian and I had to hunt in the dictionaries for translation and the spelling. It was long, hard work, but were it longer and harder, still I was ready to perform it with joy and delight, for I was free, free! And I lost no time. In a week I was off to the country to work and enjoy the beauty in the open arms of a fragrant spring.

And so I have emerged and risen — yes, I have risen eighteen hundred feet above the sea level; amidst high mountains trimmed with red, green, and yellow trees — bright like Oriental rugs. I did not feel the earth beneath me. As if on wings I walked over the infinite, sky-roofed realm of splendor, brightened with sunshine, charmed with sunsets and moonlight, filled with music of the birds and happy murmurings of the innumerable streams.

And as I stood gazing into the infinite space, as I inhaled the healthful freshness, drinking the glory that spread around me, bathing in its warmth, I kept on asking, Can this be I? And the triumphant answer rang, Yes, it is I. I, away from the dirty city, the filthy streets, diseased humanity. It was I out of the misery that ground me almost to destruction. And I wished to sing, to dance, and to pray! I wished to embrace the entire world in my ecstatic gratitude.

But something clouded the sun and struck me with reproach. I suddenly felt so narrow and selfish. Have I a right to be here, to embrace nature in full charm, to enjoy the comfort of a spacious room, and eat three healthful meals a day, — when behind me, down there in the sordid city, thousands of my sisters and brothers, my fellow workers, fellow sufferers, are toiling in the stuffy factories, are wrestling for a chance to live? In my selfish desire to lighten my own burden, which became impossible, I forgot them — and what a shame!

My heart ached in anguish, I wished to run back to them, stand among them, and rise only together with them, to make possible for all to live in the open glory of the world. And I said, "I am here only to store up health, energy, and courage; I am here to grow my wings and come back to you, to begin again the fight against the sinful injustice."

A storm gathered. Clouds thickened; the waves in the lake below were lightly swelling. Soft zephyrs played on the tree branches as on enchanting harps. All silenced in unknown expectation. I leaned my head against the window, closed my eyes, held my breath and listened. In the black silence from the depths of the wood vague echoes were moving on, growing louder, and at once a mad wind swooped through the air striking in a thousand trumpets, the trees groaned, their branches bowed low to the earth in fear. The waves in the lake foamed and rushed, struggled forward and beat against the shore. As if God himself, indignant at the earth, opened the skies, flashing angry lightning, showering and thundering. The storm fearlessly raged. It cried, it sang, it threatened, it triumphed! And my voice within was like the voice of the storm. It behooved me to sing. I no more feared a storm, for I knew that after the storm the sun must shine, and I sang — "O mighty winds, I'm one of you! My soul like yours is blazing with indignation, and like you I am wrestling for freedom! Let us then unite our voices in a mighty chorus. Let us blow and scatter our trumpets far and wide — shake up the world, smash in dust the sinful structures of present society, cleanse the earth of evil and wake the people, wake them to consciousness, appeal and sing for the glory of brotherhood, of equality and love."

The winds stilled. The storm silenced, the darkness vanished. And a bright new dawn was slowly rising from a remote corner of an infinite smooth path. It had a long, long way to travel, but it was so clear — so sure to come!

Ours is the struggle for that wonderful dawn! — and to us shall belong its glory!

THE END

APPENDIX

PROTOCOL IN THE DRESS AND WAIST INDUSTRY

(In Condensed Form)

INTRODUCTORY CLAUSE

WHEREAS on the 18th day of January, 1913, the Dress and Waist Manufacturers' Association and the International Ladies' Garment Workers' Union entered into an agreement in writing, which agreement had for its object to establish just and fair standards and working conditions in the dress and waist industry and to adjust the relations between employers and workers on a basis of fairness and mutual helpfulness; and

WHEREAS the said agreement was made to run for an unlimited period and contains specific provisions for revising its terms from time to time to meet the changing requirements of the industry; and

WHEREAS the parties have held conferences with reference to amending said agreement in the respects of standards of work and compensation and machinery for making more effective the enforcement of the provisions of said agreement; and

WHEREAS the parties having agreed in conference upon certain amendments and having failed to agree upon others, and pursuant to the provisions of said agreement having submitted their differences to the Board of Arbitration constituted thereunder for final determination, and said Board having made such determinations from time to time;

NOW, THEREFORE, for the purpose of making such amendments and awards in the form of an amended and revised agreement, it is

ORDERED that the terms and conditions of such agreement as so revised and amended shall, together with the foregoing preamble, read as follows: —

The said Dress and Waist Manufacturers' Association and the International Ladies' Garment Workers' Union reaffirm the principles set forth in the original protocol of agreement above mentioned and the contractual terms of the said agreement are modified and amended to read as follows: —

TERMS OF EMPLOYMENT AND SHOP STANDARDS

A. Wages

Week-Workers. The following shall be the minimum rates for week-workers: —

1. *Provisions relating to Cutters, including Apprentices*

Full-fledged cutters who have heretofore been receiving a minimum of $25 per week, $27.50 (men only).

Cutters' apprentices are divided into four grades: —

Grade A, $6.00; Grade B, $12.00; Grade C, $18.00; Grade D, $21.00.

2. Drapers (women only), $15.00.
3. Joiners (women only), 13.00.
4. Sample-makers (women only), $15.00.
5. Examiners (women only), $11.50.
6. Finishers (women only), $9.50.
7. Ironers (women), $14.00.
8. Ironers (men), $17.00.
9. Pressers (men), $23.00.
10. Cleaners: Girls under 16, during the first year, $6.00; girls 16 or over, during the first year, $7.00; girls under 16, during the second year, $7.00; girls 16 or over, during the second year, $8.50.

A piece-rate for operators shall be fixed on a basis which will yield to an average experienced worker not less than thirty-five (35) cents for each hour of continuous work.

Test Shop

1. There shall be established and put into immediate operation under the supervision of the Board of Protocol Standards, a Test Shop under the direction and management of a competent, practical, and impartial director, for the

purpose of ascertaining what is a fair working schedule rate to be fixed for any part of a garment in any factory, in case of dispute between employer and worker.

2. The cost of maintaining and operating the Test Shop shall be fixed by the Joint Board of Protocol Standards and shall be borne jointly by the Association and the Union.

WORK TIME

1. *Hours of Labor.* A week's work shall consist of forty-nine (49) hours in six working days. Work shall not begin before 8 A.M. and shall not continue after 6 P.M. on week days nor after 1 P.M. on Saturdays or Sundays.

2. Workers observing Saturdays may work on Sundays instead.

3. The following six legal holidays shall be observed in the industry: Washington's Birthday, Decoration Day, Independence Day, Labor Day, Thanksgiving Day, and Christmas. All workers shall be paid full wages for such holidays.

4. Overtime work shall be strictly limited to five hours in any one week and one hour on any one day except on Saturdays and Sundays, in cases of emergency.

PAY FOR OVERTIME

1. All week-workers shall receive double rate of pay for overtime work.

2. All piece-workers shall receive extra compensation for overtime on the basis of the base rate fixed for a worker of average skill and experience.

HOME WORK

1. No work shall be given to workers to be performed at their homes.

DISCRIMINATION AND DISCHARGES

1. All employees shall be duly safeguarded against unfair and wrongful discharges and against oppressive exercise by the employer of his functions in connection with all dealings with the workers.

2. No employee shall be discharged or discriminated against on the ground of his direct or indirect participation in Union activities.

3. The employer is entirely free to select his employees at his discretion, free to discharge the incompetent, the insubordinate, the inefficient, those unsuited to the work in the shop, those subversive of order and harmony in the shop and those unfaithful to their obligations. He is free, in good faith, to reorganize his shop whenever, in his judgment, the conditions of business should make it necessary for him to do so, and he is free to assign work requiring a superior or special kind of skill to those employees who possess the requisite skill.

Preferential Union Shop

1. Each member of the Association shall maintain a Union shop, that being understood to mean a shop in which protocol standards as to safety and sanitation and as to working conditions, hours of labor, and rate of wages as herein stipulated, prevail, and in which Union members shall be preferred in the hiring, employing, and retaining of help and in the distribution of work.

Board of Arbitration

1. There shall be a Board of Arbitration in the industry, composed of three persons, one to be selected by the Association, one by the Union, and one representing the public.

METHODS FOR ENFORCEMENT OF STANDARDS THROUGHOUT THE INDUSTRY

Joint Board of Sanitary Control

1. The Joint Board of Sanitary Control established in the dress and waist industry shall be continued and the parties agree, as heretofore, that said Board shall be empowered to establish standards of sanitary conditions and conditions of safety, to which the Manufacturers' Association and the Union shall be committed.

BOARD OF PROTOCOL STANDARDS

1. Recognizing the difficulties of imposing high standards of wages and working conditions upon members of the Association and the difficulty of maintaining such standards for the workers in the shops of such members, and for the purpose of carrying out the pledge of the parties to equalize standards of working conditions throughout the industry, both organizations do now agree to establish a joint board for the establishment and enforcement of such standards, to be known as the Board of Protocol Standards.

WHITE PROTOCOL LABEL

1. To make more effective the maintenance of sanitary conditions throughout the industry, to insure the equality or minimum standard throughout the industry, and to guarantee to the public garments made in shops certified by the Board of Sanitary Control, the parties agree that there shall be instituted in the industry a system of certificating garments by label to be affixed to the garment.

www.ingramcontent.com/pod-product-compliance
Lightning Source LLC
LaVergne TN
LVHW020211110826
845151LV00003B/675

* 9 7 8 1 4 2 5 5 3 6 0 8 4 *